The Process of Improvement

Every Organization's
Step-By-Step Guide to
Achieving Radically
Improved Results

Vaughn Thurman

FREILING
AGENCY

Published by Freiling Agency, LLC.

P.O. Box 1264
Warrenton, VA 20188

www.FreilingAgency.com

PB ISBN: 978-1-963701-88-3
E-book ISBN: 978-1-963701-91-3

TABLE OF CONTENTS

ACKNOWLEDGMENTS

The author would like to acknowledge HighGear's wonderful customers, without whom we would have never learned many of the best practices we share in this book. Among those, the most important were our early adopters, including some of the world's largest financial services organizations, energy producers, government agencies, and the professionals who make those organizations run. Those early adopters could see that we were on to something and were willing to risk learning together with a small upstart to leverage the advantage we were building. I would also be remiss if I failed to credit the excellent team of professionals at HighGear for their efforts to learn from our clients and to use that knowledge to improve our product and best practices with that knowledge continuously.

Specifically, I would like to acknowledge Josh Yeager, Matt Rodenbaugh, Josh Cales, John Barr, Matthew Rodatus, Mark Porter, Brandon Grimes, and the many others who supported this effort by contributing so much to the content and vision for this book.

INTRODUCTION

From the vast darkness of the ocean, a coral larva floats to the surface, seeking the light. For weeks, it is tossed aimlessly about the waves, from current to current, until it opportunistically happens upon an available rock. What happens next is both coincidence and miracle, as our larva and its rock transform into a small yet sophisticated colony. As time passes, additional larvae arrive, and the colony grows, becoming infinitely more intricate and connected. Plant life flourishes, countless animal species move in, predators begin to hunt, and what started as a chance process between a larva needing a home and a stable rock emerges into an incredibly diverse and complex ecosystem, a bit like a tiny universe.

Much like the coral reef, organizations also have foundational and emergent processes. When it is just the founder and her first assistant processing mortgages, the founder talks to the prospect, and the assistant knows precisely how to get the client's paperwork together. They file all the information in a common filing cabinet. That first filing cabinet becomes their 'coral reefs' bedrock. This small team can quickly find all the information needed to keep things moving in that filing cabinet. Later, when they hire a third person to share their work, the new team member won't be familiar with the filing system. They will also be responsible for gathering customers' financial data, and they will place this information into a new additional filing cabinet. Add five years and ten more people, and our example organization has now evolved into that coral reef of interconnected and organically developed processes built one atop the other.

These "emergent" processes are often sufficient up until a certain point. The challenge arises when the world discovers your now-refined offering, and the organization must scale up quickly and hire more people to meet the demand. It becomes critical to smooth out the complexity of operations to deliver a more consistent customer experience at scale. The organization must increase efficiency to keep the complexities of scale from undermining growth. At this point, process becomes an asset for some and a liability for others. Why?

> *Process Maturity* measures the level at which firms have learned to embrace, define, document, and continuously refine processes to scale and standardize outcomes.

According to a [1]Deloitte Survey in 2020, process-mature organizations, no matter their size, were growing roughly three times faster and more sustainably than their competitors who lacked process maturity. That is because good processes reduce chaos. That will lead to more effective recruiting and talent retention because the best people are attracted to well-run organizations, and better teams provide superior outcomes for their stakeholders. In a hyper-competitive world, intent matters, execution is critical, but outcomes matter most.

If you think that process improvement is a tedious, low-value activity reserved for the back office of companies with too many people on their payroll, you have it all wrong. Process is the enabler of consistent delivery, and consistent delivery across time separates winners from losers. You will

---

[1] https://www2.deloitte.com/us/en/insights/topics/digital-transformation/digital-transformation-survey.html

either embrace process improvement, or you will eventually be defeated by your competitors that do.

This book will teach anyone how to effectively champion and execute change within their organizations. First, it will provide empirical data regarding the significant and sustainable advantages process improvement conveys to the organizations that embrace it. Second, it tackles eliminating the complexity, drudgery, and friction typically associated with process improvement efforts by examining where, how, and why most process improvement efforts fail. Finally, a step-by-step guide leads you through your effort to improve the processes through which things get done.

PART ONE

WHY PROCESS MATTERS

CHAPTER ONE

THE POWER OF PROCESS: WHY PROCESS-BASED BUSINESSES WIN AND WIN BIG

"When the going gets tough, the tough get going!"
—Joe Scherrer, The Corpus Christi Times, 1953

That often-overused saying may have more truth to it than you would expect. In 2020, at the start of a worldwide economic shock, Deloitte published research showing that companies with a higher *digital maturity* rating reported an average of 45% revenue growth compared to an average of 15% for companies with lower maturity rankings.[2] Think about that for a moment. Would most organizations expect a measurable 3X advantage just by investing in improving and streamlining processes using digital technology? Over a decade, that kind of advantage will make the difference between the leaders of a market and those who face the crushing weight of an outsized competitor.

Let's consider two equally sized companies starting that decade with $100M in revenue. In ten years, the one growing at a 15% compounding rate will have reached $404M in revenue. That's impressive growth! However, their competitor,

---

[2] https://www2.deloitte.com/content/dam/insights/us/articles/6561_digital-transformation/DI_Digital-transformation.pdf

growing at a 45% compounded rate, will have reached $4.1B in annual revenue simultaneously.

In our simple example, the smaller company will now have to defend itself in a market where its dominant competitor has scaled up to ten times their size. That likely means the larger competitor has ten times the marketing budget, ten times the sales force, ten times the locations and services, and ten times the ability to deliver. That is an overwhelming advantage that can reasonably be traced back to the decision made by that organization a decade earlier to invest in digitizing its processes and workflow.

> *Digital Maturity* reflects the level at which an organization has embraced digitization of the elements and artifacts of their work to standardize their outcomes, and it necessarily includes process maturity.

That is a staggering difference to attribute to digital transformation. You might ask, "But how does that digital maturity rating equate to organizational process?" Let's consider for a minute what "process" is:

Process is the coherent movement of information and artifacts associated with a transaction intended to produce or deliver a desired result.

The benefits of process are not just financial. According to a report by McKinsey & Company, companies that focus on process improvement and automation can achieve 20-50% higher productivity levels than their peers.[3] Process-based

---

[3] https://www.mckinsey.com/capabilities/operations/our-insights/operations-blog/have-you-fully-cracked-the-efficiency-code

businesses have typically experienced the upside that can be unlocked by focusing on streamlining and optimizing operations. Well-defined procedures lead to well-defined and predictable outcomes, and when measured against a baseline, the virtuous investment cycle begins. Process-savvy organizations achieve higher efficiency and productivity by eliminating bottlenecks, reducing waste, and standardizing workflows. That means less chaos, which leads to happier employees. Human nature and firsthand experience tell us that a business with happy employees has a far easier time producing happy customers.

Manual processes are fraught with human error; often, simply finding where that error occurred can be cumbersome. Records must be retrieved from human memories or filing cabinets, possibly in distant locations, and then reviewed by other humans, now discouraged by the struggle and low value of trying to find and fix poor-quality work. Simply digitizing the collection of information can be called digital transformation, but that is also undoubtedly the lowest definition.

Manual processes may be as basic as writing an order down on a pad of paper and sending that order to an inventory clerk for fulfillment, taking an inbound call and filling out a paper form, or adding a line to a shared spreadsheet to represent that client's requested change. However, manual processes may also include far more sophisticated work, like onboarding a large-scale investment client, where numerous disclosures must be presented, signed, and properly filed, or specific documents must be completed to meet the bare minimum of regulatory requirements. Yet all these offer the potential for compounding benefits when digital transformation is applied.

The steps in these varied examples all require or infer subject matter expertise that can be digitized. Consider the simple example of a person taking an order. What goods or services can the client order? Consider the person or team filing regulatory documents that must follow the rules precisely. Who can or should be able to retrieve these needed items, and where should they be filed? Consider the regulatory team and their process controls. How do we ensure that the aggregated data from these forms are submitted to regulators accurately and filed before the legal deadlines? And further, how can we prove how and when these tasks were done?

Multi-department or multi-discipline processes often route work, transactions, orders, and other artifacts across multiple specialized teams or disciplines. For instance, after onboarding an investment fund client, records may need to be reviewed by a quality assurance team, who in turn may need to report exceptions or problems to a legal team, a compliance team, or a customer service team (or all of them) for additional corrections or review. Those later reviews may require further cross-departmental approvals and signoffs to show that the policies and regulations for dealing with exceptions were also complied with.

A study by the American Productivity and Quality Center (APQC - apqc.org) found that process-focused companies spend 35% less on their core business processes than those neglecting process improvement.

Sophisticated and rules-based streams of work like this cannot simply be digitized (i.e., the simplest act of digital transformation) or moved "from paper to a database" without first engaging and leveraging an organization's subject matter expertise, details of precision, and process controls to assure the intended outcomes and compliance. All these ingredients are required for digital transformation efforts to succeed. Ultimately, whether it be the client interacting with a web or mobile form, a customer service person reviewing a request, or a legal subject matter expert contributing to the final result, one truth remains. Digital transformation, on its own, does not change what work is done. Digital transformation only changes how the information and artifacts are conveyed and how quickly and easily they can be analyzed or reviewed later.

Digital transformation's core objective is this: That processes become more agile, repeatable, visible, and traceable by eliminating manual work and artifacts like paper, email, sticky notes, and inconsistent data.

The [4]American Society for Quality reports a positive correlation between effective process management and improved customer satisfaction. Implementing effective processes allows organizations to achieve greater consistency and quality in their products or services. Process-based businesses reduce variations and errors by standardizing procedures and implementing quality control measures, leading to higher customer satisfaction and loyalty.

We started with the recognition that effectively digitizing processes can lead to a massive organizational advantage over a handful of years. That advantage can be traced back to the organizationally curious individual who first wondered, "Could we make this run better?"

Digital transformation is accomplished by digitizing the forms, files, and other supporting artifacts flowing through your process. When done well, this effort unlocks an acceleration of subsequent process improvements because of the inherent ability of *agile* digital systems to improve the quality of incoming information incrementally, increasing data consistency across the board. Data consistency makes it easier to analyze process bottlenecks and opportunities, thus facilitating faster and more beneficial subsequent incremental

---

[4] asq.org

changes. Meanwhile, at the other end of the continuum, where digital transformation has been executed poorly using rigid or brittle systems and technology, problems in the physical realm can easily migrate to the digital realm, where they may become even more expensive and difficult to correct.

Beneficial workarounds are on-the-fly alternative ways of getting something done when systems are broken or deficient. While pragmatically creative results-focused contributors could easily and quickly implement real-world workarounds, traditional brittle systems will require the help of specialized IT personnel to do that same thing in the digital world. That is, if they are even available. We will expound upon this problem, its root causes, and how to solve both later.

But let's get back to the question implied at the beginning of this section, "Why does this book claim that digital transformation is all about process?" The answer is that, at the heart of digital transformation, we find the processes, tasks, workflows, approvals, escalations, rules, audit trails, and all the other elements that once comprised manual or paper processes and their associated artifacts. These are the things to be digitized.

Process-mature, process-aware, and process-ready organizations (all of which we will further define later) are better prepared to achieve digital transformation out of the gate. If they have paired that organizational capability with agile technology, they will *continue* to accelerate ahead of their less mature peers because the processes they are changing already reside in the digital domain. Agility is the foundation they will build upon. An organization must understand process improvement and the potential pitfalls of digitizing broken processes or implementing them through brittle technologies.

Organizations that do not understand or adequately value "process improvement" may find digital transformation efforts painful, slow, fraught with errors, and underwhelming in their outcomes.

So far, we've considered the linear benefits of starting and embracing process change across time. Still, another set of critical advantages for companies that have already embraced digital transformation are the twin sisters of Agility and Adaptability. Agility and adaptability are crucial for success in today's rapidly changing business landscape. As organizations grow, process-based businesses that insist on digitizing work *within* agile platforms will be better equipped to respond to unexpected market dynamics. Well-defined processes, implemented in systems that are easy and safe to change, enable organizations to quickly adapt operations, onboard employees, and introduce new products or services. Less agile competitors will still discuss the risks of change while the savvy firm has already made the needed change and begins leveraging its agility dividend.

Additionally, a business that deploys and expands strong automated controls reduces the risks of business-crushing events such as publicized data breaches, embezzlement, misuse of funds, improperly approved expenditures, and lawsuits.

The choice should be clear, given the many advantages available to the process-based organization and the many disadvantages faced by those who fall behind. If you have not already started your process-improvement journey, consider this axiom: The best time to start doing the right thing was yesterday, but the second-best time is today.

One question we often hear in corporate circles is, "Shouldn't we wait until we have chosen a technology platform to start working on process improvement?" The short and definitive answer is no.

Suppose two companies undertake digital transformation at the same time. In that case, the organization that already excels at process improvement in the physical realm will have a distinct advantage over the competitor who lacks process savvy, even if the latter has a substantially larger technology budget.

Regardless of your technology decisions, the steps you can take include the same *Four D's* that make up rapid process improvement in the technology space: *Discovery, Design, Documentation, and Deployment.* While these steps may all be more rapid, effective, scalable, and agile if they are happening within the *right* technology stack, the fundamentals, as we will discuss within this book, remain the same.

Building process improvement disciplines into your corporate mindset early will always be beneficial. New information bubbles up frequently in an agile process improvement effort. Understanding this before a team selects technology will help that team know why they must achieve a similar or greater level of agility when they are ready to migrate their processes to the digital realm.

The Small Business Advantage

You may want to skip this section if you manage or work for a business with over 500 employees. However, if someone in your family owns or is considering starting a small business, I encourage you to read on. You may be surprised to learn that there are tremendous opportunities available within the area of process improvement for small businesses.

Small business owners often think that process won't help them until they get bigger. However, the truth is that small businesses that embrace process will have an easier time scaling, while process-immature businesses may never catch up.

According to a Harvard Business Review article titled [5] "A Way Forward for Small Businesses," small businesses with

---

[5] https://hbr.org/2020/04/a-way-forward-for-small-businesses or https://web.archive.org/web/20230324142849/https://cdn.advocacy.sba.gov/wp-content/uploads/2018/12/21060437/Small-Business-GDP-1998-2014.pdf

fewer than 500 employees account for 48% of American jobs and 43.5% of GDP.

Numerically, small businesses are America's most significant business category! They should embrace their leadership opportunity by building process into everything they do from the ground up. However, though most realize process improvements could help them, they often find themselves trapped in a resource conundrum. Lacking their larger counterparts' available time, capacity, finances, and staffing, they wonder if they can afford to slow down to speed up. Many small business leaders don't realize that if they implement a state-of-the-art process, the outcomes will be transformational and likely free up their personnel to accomplish more high-value work, including additional process improvements.

The fact that small businesses exist at all is proof that the market wants what small business delivers best. That is accountability! [6]A Gallup poll in 2021 showed that small businesses, in general, were viewed favorably by 97% of those surveyed. That was one of the top categories and starkly contrasted large organizations and other "top" performers like the U.S. Government, scoring a paltry 38%. The reasons cited included accountability and personal service. People know that large businesses can make massive mistakes, deliver consistently poor service, and survive by volume, market share, or the lack of viable alternatives. On the other hand, they know that small businesses depend on each sale and the impression they make in each customer interaction. Small companies are typically regional, where reputations are crucial.

---

[6] https://news.gallup.com/poll/5248/big-business.aspx
Question: Just off the top of your head, would you say you have a positive or negative image of each of the following?
⁻ Small Business 97, Big Business 46, U.S. Government 38

The market's general trust for small businesses is not poorly placed. After all, the consumer sentiment described above is reasonably accurate. A small business that has survived a handful of years either came out of the gates with good customer service or quickly learned to provide it. Otherwise, they would already be out of business. This trust will allow a small business to compete with large companies effectively. For instance, people will assume that a national chain that installs automobile tires will be less likely to resolve an issue for an unsatisfied customer than a small business. This general axiom is not always true, but it is often enough to give small businesses a leg up when competing with that national chain.

However, if you have three local small businesses to choose from, they will all benefit from that same trust. With the associated trust being equal for all three, each business will now have to compete on:

- Reputation,
- Value (quality, consistency, and availability of the goods and services provided), and
- Price (of course)!

Considering the inherent accountability of small businesses, it is reasonable to assume that these local providers, having been in business for any length of time, will all have worked at having a good reputation. That means they are down to two categories upon which they can still truly compete:

- Value (quality, consistency, and speed of the goods and services provided)
- Price.

If you run a small business and find that your primary means of competing is price, you had better have sophisticated cost control mechanisms available. The problem is that many of the best cost control levers are not typically available to small businesses because of their lower volumes. In other words, the reality is that whether you choose it or not, the competitive area over which you can exercise the most control is the delivery of goods and services.

Each transaction is a process. Getting your business open each morning is a process. Getting it closed each night and making the bank deposits is a process. Hiring the right people is a process, or at least it should be! Onboarding and training those people are processes. Ensuring your customers are satisfied with what they have received is a process. Those processes may be haphazard or polished. They may be designed or organic. They may be well documented, or they may all be living in the heads of your staff.

The simple rules you implement as your business evolves, such as 'let's call every 10th customer and see if they were happy', must also be monitored somehow, or they are likely to dissipate or fail.

> *A vision without a plan is just a daydream.*
> —Paul Foss

Small businesses that take on process improvement as an ongoing part of their business will always enjoy an advantage. While small companies typically have less automation and less middle management to enforce policy, they also often enjoy higher employee engagement. That means that, generally, small business employees want to do the right thing. However, that also means that the consistency of delivery will be constrained by the consistency of training or the communication and administration of policies – i.e., policy controls.

The small business that gets out in front of this and assumes that developing process and process controls is as ordinary a part of growing a business as moving to a new office when they have outgrown one will find themselves reaping dividends over time. Employee turnover is a certainty. If a company is growing, adding new employees is a certainty. What is not certain is that these new employees will know how to do what you promised your customers you would do. Experienced employees intuitively know how to solve problems when something goes wrong, but new employees might not. It might seem basic, but simply documenting the rules around problem-solving and empowering your newer or less creative employees to repeat the best practices of experienced employees and business leaders is, in fact, process improvement.

Stage one of process improvement for a small business is simply interviewing a team about how things are getting done and then standardizing those best practices into documented and communicated processes.

Stage two of process improvement for a small business is having someone who understands the business proactively study how things get done while looking for potential optimizations, shortcuts, or ways to deliver compelling or differentiated customer experiences. Examples of how this can be accomplished include shopping a competitor, traveling to another city and seeing how similar businesses are run in another region, or having friends, family, or consultants mystery shop your business with fresh eyes.

Stage three of process improvement for a small business is to determine what parts of any of these interactions or transactions can be improved and documented. Or better yet, how they can be automated or facilitated by technology.

What does it mean for a process to be automated? While it may mean no further human interaction will be required, that is not typically the case. In a practical sense, "process automation" involves capturing, routing, displaying, and analyzing the information and artifacts that make up a transaction. For a small business, the entrepreneur is often the process expert. They know from experience exactly what information must be captured from each client or prospective client. However, new people will not have that experience as the business grows and will not intuitively understand the ramifications of failing to clarify the necessary details upfront. Problems will emerge downstream because insufficient information is captured during each transaction. That is process failure. Automating the process to ensure that a transaction cannot be accepted without all the necessary information is an example of process control.

Computer facilitation could be as simple as taking a paper document (with four highlighted fields to be filled out to benefit a customer service rep who will submit a new work order) and migrating that form into a computer system for data entry through a device. That digitized form now *ensures* those fields are filled out before the work order can be accepted, a basic example of a technical process control.

Zoom out, and we will see that most small businesses do some level of process improvement along the way. However, most do it in reaction to things that go wrong. Thus, every time they make a process improvement, they do it at the expense of a potentially unhappy customer, frustrated employee, or an economic loss associated with a troubled transaction.

Small businesses that embrace process improvement as a proactive effort find that they can incrementally improve their business operation while also avoiding the risks their competitors face. As the consistency of their delivery continually improves, their competitor plays catch up, still reacting to errors and problems.

The earlier a small business moves towards digital transformation (the automation and computer facilitation of its processes), the sooner it will have a growing library of easily searched and analyzed historical records that enable it to continue the virtuous cycle of looking for areas where those same processes can be further improved. Meanwhile, their competitor, who redesigned a paper form and trained their employees on using the "new and improved paper form," finds itself hiring new employees unaware that the "pink" fields are required, and the failure cycle repeats.

Technical process control delivers an advantage for small business leaders who have embraced process improvement and evolutionary digital transformation as they go.

According to the [7]'Small Business Digitalization and COVID-19' Survey of June 2020, small businesses engaged in digital transformation saw eight times the revenue growth of those without digital efforts. That is one of many studies showing that process and technology maturity are market equalizers, allowing small businesses to lead and overtake their larger competitors. However, a stumbling block can arise for smaller firms when leadership allocates people resources but does not have the time necessary to complete transformation projects successfully. With less of a resource pool to draw on, unexpected personnel changes can be the root cause of this lack of follow-through. In other words, the small business leader may intend to see a digital or process transformation

---

[7] https://www.cisco.com/c/dam/en_us/solutions/small-business/resource-center/small-business-digital-transformation.pdf

through, but losing key personnel can derail the progress. That highlights and amplifies the need for small businesses to be even more aggressive about demanding agility from the systems and technologies they will use to digitize their operations. Modern choices like configurable software or no-code platforms can help mitigate these risks that are more of a threat to small businesses.

The Big Business Advantage

Big businesses often fail because they believe their size makes them safe. Jim Collins's book, "How the Mighty Fall," examines that phenomenon in great detail. That book is one of a series of three: **Good to Great, Great by Choice**, and **How the Mighty Fall**. These three books comprise some of the best modern studies of a wide range of businesses. The overarching goal of Collin's research was to identify what led to the success or failure of the companies he and his research teams studied.

Each of those three books is worth the time one would invest in reading them. A key lesson in all three books is that size is not an advantage for a business unless that size is continuously leveraged to create and maintain an advantage. It may take longer for a large company to realize that it is losing out to a smaller competitor with superior products or services, and that may feel like safety, but it is also a vulnerability.

If a smaller competitor has a better offering in the market, it may take a long time for that smaller competitor to scale up enough to be noticed by its larger competitor. However, when the larger competitor notices the threat, the smaller competitor will already have momentum. The larger competitor will suffer a significant disadvantage due to the time required for a large organization to pivot and respond to the input it is now receiving from the market. Meanwhile, smaller companies with superior offerings will continue to accelerate while larger and heavier competitors will slow down before they can turn.

The idea of the fast overtaking the slow is not just theory. As we have described, small companies that can deliver superior customer experiences frequently overtake larger companies while their lumbering competition struggles. Smaller businesses often lack the optimized processes that once made larger competitors so hard to attack. Still, having become inflexible and rigid, those same processes have become the larger firm's Achilles heel. In contrast, large businesses that embrace constant process improvement (e.g., Amazon's innovation teams) and work to keep their processes pliable make it nearly impossible for their smaller competitors to ever catch up. The point? Large businesses should regard their size as an opportunity to invest in process and further embrace that process advantage as the only sustainable way to maintain distance between themselves and their less-resourced but lighter and faster competitors.

Of course, this kind of innovation and change is more complex for a large business. In a large company, a vital part of a process may be performed by 100 people across a department. Therefore, you cannot change a process as quickly as running down the hallway and telling "Peter" the new way we must file the TPS reports (Don't forget the cover page!). Large businesses may have employees working in different shifts, locations, and languages. As a result, there are more considerations associated with change. That complexity factor will accentuate the need for agility.

Generating, preserving, and ferociously defending agility is a greater necessity for a large organization that wants to stay ahead of leaner competitors. Sometimes, the careful consideration of change is a necessary burden that comes with scale. Compliance requirements may also be a significant, unavoidable cost for a larger business. Overlaying regulatory and other forms of compliance means that agility will be more complex and must be deliberately created and maintained in innovative areas. However, this is also where big businesses have a genuine advantage. They have the resources (expertise, human resources, and capital) necessary to pursue the most agile technologies, the most experienced change management professionals, and teams of bright business analysts.

Resources: Software Development (programmers) vs. Software Configuration (business analysts)

You may notice that the list of human resources an organization could recruit to aid its process improvement efforts failed to include programmers. It was by design. They are a needed resource, but they are also expensive and increasingly rare, especially the ones that understand your business. That is not to say that programmers are not valuable. Instead, they should focus on the areas where they can deliver the most impact because of their significant value.

Asking your business users for the names of the fields they want on a new form is not a good use of a programmer's specialized skills. Writing code to ensure customers can't accidentally type dollar amounts in a Project Due Date field has the same problem. Configuring a dashboard that presents tasks to workers isn't a good use of their time either. Building a simple chart showing a manager the status of various items moving through their business process no longer warrants a programmer. All these things are essential, but modern agile technologies, now within reach of businesses of all sizes, enable analysts to do these things themselves without writing code. So why on earth would we have strategically valuable and relatively expensive programmers doing any of those things?

Keep your innovators innovating and your organizers organizing.

Programmers. Programmers (software engineers or developers, as you may prefer to call them) are our modern architects, engineers, and builders. They should be working on technical innovation. Technical innovation is not equivalent to process orchestration. Process orchestration is innovation, but it is the innovation of *how* you do things. Technical innovation involving developers should be about creating and building altogether new ways of delivering goods and services to clients. Developers are also particularly useful at connecting existing applications and building frameworks to provide rapid decision support to your stakeholders, such as customers, staff members, managers, or even your Board of Directors. If you are running a large business, keep your innovators innovating and keep your organizers organizing.

Business Analysts. Few people who run small businesses recognize the title "business analyst." Yet, most mid- to large-size businesses already employ them. They wear many hats and have many titles. A VP of Operations may be a highly experienced business analyst. Other business analysts may have titles such as medical analyst, finance analyst, process analyst, or credit analyst. However, while many small business leaders are unfamiliar with the title, they have probably nonetheless learned to value and seek out people with those skills.

So, let's stop and define what a business analyst is. A business analyst is someone who… well… analyzes business. That may seem a bit simplistic, but it isn't. A good business analyst:

- Knows how to ask practical and efficient questions that lead to quickly understanding how a business unit performs work and the information and artifacts it needs to keep that work flowing
- Identifies opportunities for optimization
- Practically envisions how work can be done more effectively
- Records solution requirements harvested from the business units and leaders they interview
- **In the old model,** they would convey their requirements for new or improved solutions to programmers, software engineers, or developers.

The old model should call to mind the childhood game "telephone," where someone whispers something into one person's ear and it goes around the room only to become something often comically different. However, when these digital transformation projects have budgets in the millions of dollars and take many months or years to complete, the results of that game of telephone lack a comedic crescendo. It's just not as funny when it costs you a lot of money and may also cost you your job.

The new model involves empowering business analysts (and people who think like them), whenever and wherever possible, to configure and deploy the solutions they can envision quickly, securely, and autonomously.

Today, most business analysts act as the go-between for the business units with digital transformation needs and the software development teams, who increasingly have less time to address them. While the skills and experience of a business analyst are invaluable, they are often left unable to convert their detailed plans and beneficial insights into reality.

Forward-thinking large businesses will see business analysts as their wormhole (or technology-based shortcut) to the future. We will delve into this further in Chapter Six, in the Finding Your Hidden Resources section. Suppose you have staff members who are already skilled at discovering business needs and opportunities (and if you have business analysts on staff, you already do). Why not empower them with agile technologies that enable them to build secure and scalable solutions themselves? We will provide a solid body of empirical proof that organizations need this, that business analysts want to contribute in this way, and that the organizations that embrace these new philosophies can implement process improvements in far less time than those who still have their business analysts work through a software development team.

The large businesses that adopt this strategy will not only be able to pivot quickly when new competition arrives on their radar but will also have the skills and speed necessary to execute that pivot in record time without hiring an army of consultants. When a large business can respond quickly to emerging competitive threats, it can transform the disadvantage of being a late arriver into the advantage of being a better-resourced fast follower. A large business with this process agility can look at its small competitors as a free test bed. Suppose one of their competitors develops an innovative way to deliver services to the market, and the market responds favorably. In that case, they can quickly pivot and neutralize the advantage while exercising their dominance through scale.

Of course, this kind of agility requires the large organization to think and invest strategically. The belief in the existence of this advantage is not enough. The agile technologies must already be in place, and the organization must have navigated the agility adoption curve. An organization must also have ready human resources for deployment to any area of the organization that identifies a need.

As mentioned earlier, Amazon is known for deploying *innovation teams* that bring together localized subject matter experts (i.e., someone who works in the area where the problem exists), process experts, technology experts, and others identified as creative thinkers or entrepreneurial innovators. These teams gather quickly when a problem or threat is discovered. If they believe they can find a better way to do something, can figure out how to solve the problem, or can neutralize a competitive threat, then they are allowed to make changes - even rapid changes - in small areas of the business to prove their expected benefits. If they deliver the expected results, their changes can be deployed quickly across the rest of the organization.

You may or may not be a fan of Amazon, but I doubt you would want to start a business today to compete with them. Their advantage is not their size but that they have used their size to further their advantage. Even if you could raise the capital to become their equal in terms of infrastructure and manpower, the time that it would take you to hire those people and get them to work would be enough time for Amazon to further change the way they do business enough that you would be playing catch-up again the first day your doors open.

現場に行く

The Japanese phrase "going to the Gemba" is often used in process improvement. In police work, it implies "going to where the crime occurred." It is also frequently used to suggest that the most valuable information regarding how a process currently operates or could be improved can be ascertained by going to where the deed is done.

Big businesses have incredible opportunities for process improvement if they are equally committed to process agility. Process agility is rarely produced via top-down innovation. Top-down innovation may be an effective product strategy (consider Steve Jobs' unique vision for Apple or Elon Musk's specific vision for Tesla or SpaceX). Still, it is not typically an effective strategy for process. Process improvements must come from the bottom up. That is why the Japanese (who led the rest of the world in embracing lean manufacturing) use the phrase "going to the Gemba." Embedding business analysts within business units ensures that you have human resources at the ready whose competence is process awareness and process improvement. If you hire the right people, they become your champions of change when change is required.

Of course, this will also require changes in your decision-making process. If your organization makes all decisions from the top and cascades them down, an uncomfortable conversation is probably in your best interest. Senior management is typically responsible for revising a company's offering based on numerous inputs and their significant market understanding. However, the people "at the Gemba" (where the work is being done) must be involved in *how* the moving parts of an organization's processes will facilitate this change. Their critical input is rooted in their significant and localized operational understanding, and overlooking it is usually costly. Thinking and operationalizing change this way requires a shift from top-down to results-based leadership. "My team may not do it as I would, but if they can get the desired results, that's the shared goal."

Another mindset that must be conquered for a large organization to press its potential advantage is the old phrase, "That's how we have always done it." That implies no interest in changing, and many a sage will tell you, "Anything that isn't changing or growing is dying." Modern, tech-savvy workers know that to be true, and they will flee the organization that believes itself impervious to change. Your organization at all levels must adopt the idea that change is necessary and that implementing change well is how an organization will win.

Takeaways

- Small businesses have the advantage of inherent agility. Because every process is new, they can offer the opportunity for high process ownership and meaningful stakeholder feedback loops. They can press that advantage by building process design into their approach as early as possible and committing to deploying agile solutions that keep them as fast as they are fresh.

- Big businesses have the advantage of stability and resources that can be deployed against emerging threats. They can leverage that advantage by building agility into their technology, process improvement methodologies, and human capital management efforts. By adopting a bottom-up approach for process improvement and a top-down approach for market direction and product or service creation, innovative large businesses can become incredibly difficult for new or smaller competitors to catch up with.

- Process is at the root of all these advantages. Genuinely empowered people in large and small businesses will naturally help build, maintain, and press their advantage.

- People want to solve other people's problems. People inside of an organization are the same. They want to be problem solvers for the people around them. The key question is, do an organization's processes and systems help their employees solve problems, or do they force them to create workarounds outside their systems? Consider the organization that empowers its people to dynamically build and improve its processes. In this environment, stakeholders and contributors will start personally identifying with their processes and process improvements and want to prove how well they work. That virtuous cycle will attract others who want to be part of high-performance empowered teams. Innovative organizations will leverage this. These organizations must only provide the framework, governance, and empowerment for these A+ team players to innovate. Those empowered contributors will adopt and beneficially refine processes by contributing to the winning subsystems they have always longed to help create, manage, and improve.

Note: In addition to agile tools, there are also agile methodologies that can help guide a business through process improvement. These include: DMAIC, DFSS, Lean, LDfSS, Lead Six Sigma, ITIL, CMM, etc. Those philosophies and applications like HighGear are just the tools, you are still the craftsman, and the quality of the results will come from how effectively you wield the tools.

CHAPTER TWO

SMOOTH IS FAST

A business owner our team worked with proudly shared that his team "could respond to problems more rapidly than any of his competitors." That statement sounds positive. However, it was qualified by his following remark: "The unfortunate thing is that they also cause most of those problems."

He had a highly committed team who would do whatever it took to make things right for a client once those problems reached the surface. However, what his team lacked was the process to ensure that those problems never happened at all. When process is applied, there will be a cost to transactional speed. But that short-term performance hit is more than recovered by not having to do rework, the management meetings to figure out what went wrong, the calls to clients to apologize, the marketing to replace clients, or all the other things that go along with reacting under duress.

The old military line "smooth is fast" is generally true: Consistent delivery is better than fast delivery. It is better to consistently produce a predictable outcome than to rapidly produce an unpredictable outcome because unpredictable outcomes lead to exceptions.

Regardless of an organization's process maturity, exceptions will be a permanent part of any organizational reality. But there is a massive difference between handled exceptions and unhandled exceptions. For instance, imagine discovering that a financial services client does not meet the regulatory requirements of a sophisticated investor only after they have already been sold an investment that requires sophisticated investor disclosures and attestations. That is an example of an unhandled exception. The ensuing handwringing, crisis planning, and reactionary response will require the attention and involvement of senior human resources. Not only was the work of junior resources wasted by way of error, but the corrective actions are likely to be completed by senior (and thus more expensive) resources.

Consider the small business equivalent of an electrical contractor arriving at a job site to install commercial lighting. The contractor's team then discovers that the customer believed the contractor would be providing the lights while the contractor thought that the customer would be providing the lights. In this case, the time staff members spent driving to the location has been wasted. The small business will have to pay the team to return to the van and either head back to the office or go to a supply center and pick up lights, now under duress. The work schedules for the remainder of the week will also be at risk. A premium will likely be paid by the contractor, who now needs to get these lights in a hurry. The business owner will spend time on the phone learning about the error, and the disarray will negatively impact the client's perception. Field staff will have to contact the owner multiple times to get approval for specific prices or premiums to get the lights delivered quickly. Because of the rush, the employees are more likely to forget supporting materials, wiring, or connectors they may also need. The compound costs of a single miscommunication will begin to snowball quickly. Anyone who has ever run a business or team of any size can translate this example into their own situational or organizational history.

It would undoubtedly slow the intake of many simple jobs if that electrical contractor implemented controls that ensure that any employee who creates a work order must interrogate, clarify, and record specific work requirements before a work order can be placed into the schedule. Highly experienced and competent individuals often resist these kinds of controls and efforts because they seem unnecessary. That is because they are judging the value of these controls against the likelihood that they would produce this error. This thinking has two problems. First, they base their assumptions on how new employees in a growing business will function on their own past performance. Second, they are probably also overestimating their own past performance, exacerbating the first problem.

The question is, does it take more time to build the necessary process controls to ensure that the right information and artifacts are collected early, or does it take more time (and perhaps more costly time) to resolve those problems once they inevitably present themselves at the most inopportune moment? The answer should be obvious. However, it isn't evident to most people "in the thick of it." In the heat of the moment, the emotional answer is to yell, fire someone, or mutter under your breath about the difficulty of finding "good help." It goes back to the illustration we used earlier in the book of the person who is too busy to fix the square-wheeled wheelbarrow. We all find that funny and imagine it being someone else, but in the real world, it is usually us.

While it is always good for an organization to have senior people who are capable of agile and thoughtful responses to unexpected problems, the way to scale up an organization is to moderately slow down the intake of a process by requiring the specific information that is necessary for success, even if that information might not be needed for senior employees.

Rather than relying on human competence, these controls will ensure the highest probability of consistent delivery.

Let's define consistent delivery. It doesn't mean you will produce the same thing every time. A discrete manufacturing company may have a series of tools, machinery, and capabilities that it uniquely employs daily to make a new customized product. Nonetheless, what they are doing every day is the same. They use the same tools, machinery, and capabilities to produce yet another "customized product." So, in this case, we are not talking about a rigid rubberstamping process but a process within which the variables can be ascertained and further evaluated so that the delivery of a variable product or service will consistently meet the following objective outcomes:

- The product was delivered on time.
- The product met or exceeded the original requirements.
- The number of items produced (without defects) equals the number of ordered items.
- If there were any exceptions or delays, the customer was well informed of any impacts in advance.
- If changes were requested, they were documented and approved by the appropriate parties. Further, if those changes impacted cost, delivery time, quality, or the schedules for other work, those outcomes were disclosed and approved in advance.

Perhaps you've dealt with a firm that asked you many clarifying questions before they began a project for you. For example, at risk of mild annoyance, they may have asked you if your driveway was level or if the refrigerator they would be replacing already had a water hookup. Suppose they asked you those questions to confirm they understood your expectations and the environment they would be delivering to. In that case, you would likely consider that a good experience. While many subjective things go into a good experience, it is an objective statement that if you did not get what you paid for or did not get it on time, it is unlikely that you will consider that a good experience even if the people that you dealt with were delightful.

Carl Sewell's famous book "Customers for Life" spends a great deal of time talking about the importance of systems over smiles. Smiles are vital to any customer experience, but they are secondary. They are only valuable if an organization has been able to deliver what they promised. And, if they want to keep their customers for the long haul, they had better be able to deliver consistently. That requires that either every customer interaction is performed by an expert or that the organization has built that expertise into their systems to empower entry-, mid-, or senior-level employees to deliver the same outcome by controlling the intake, management, and delivery of customer requirements from end-to-end.

That being said, exceptions are a part of the reality we all live in. Process controls, a key part of process improvement, are all about eliminating as many exceptions as possible by ensuring we have gathered the data necessary to eliminate those exceptions likely to arise from human error or miscommunication. However, no matter the level of control we aspire to or achieve, we will never eliminate all exceptions.

Let's go back to our simple example of the electrical contractor. Having had that terrible experience of wasting time trying to get lights in a hurry for a project where something was miscommunicated, our theoretical electrical contractor may have quickly put in process controls to ensure that employees ask, "Will you be providing the items we are to install, or do you want us to provide them?" That may eliminate the risk of miscommunication but not the risk of a customer who has provided lights of the wrong type or voltage. If that unforeseen exception happens, they would likely return to the process canvas and modify their intake form to ask questions about the type and voltage. Problem solved! But not so fast... Perhaps the next time, they will bring white lights only to discover that their perception of white is different than their customer's perception of white. Again, exceptions will be a part of human interactions, no matter what level of control we apply.

Therein lies the reason that agile exception management becomes critical to consistent delivery. Remember, our definition of consistent delivery includes the management of change and the communication of revised expectations. No process will ever mitigate all exceptions.

The ability to handle exceptions well is often more critical than reducing their incidence. Example: One awful experience may be communicated to EVERYONE, but one well-handled problem may also reassure thousands of other buyers. Consider when you have seen a negative product review among generally positive reviews. If it says, "I was not happy with the item, but I have to admit, the vendor jumped right on it and refunded my money." Or "They sent me another one right away," doesn't that kind of feedback increase your confidence in the product or vendor?

Another critical part of exception management is agility. Rigid systems encumber agile employees and make it difficult for them to recover from the unexpected. At HighGear, when we teach people our best practices for process discovery and design, we often discuss "on-ramps" and "off-ramps." These terms are metaphors for giving people a traceable pathway for dealing with exceptions by jumping into a process at some midpoint or temporarily jumping out of a process when an unexpected exception arises. Building this kind of atypical flexibility into a process or solution design may seem scary to some who prefer the centralized control of a rigid system. However, the reality remains that agile employees will simply work around a rigid system. Your systems should allow them to exit the rigid part of a process (traceably) to effectively deal with an exception and then reenter that rigid process once the exception has been handled. The unfortunate alternative is finding your team regularly working 'outside the system' to get things done. That introduces procedural risk and reduces your real-time system to a state where data now gets entered after the fact.

This kind of rearview visibility is perilous because it dramatically reduces the ability to monitor and control work in progress. It is critical to set systems up with rigid controls around what you empirically know so far but to leave breathing room around the things you are not yet confident you know or that you cannot yet prove you know. In other words, you may be certain that when onboarding your new financial services client, you will need their name, address, telephone number, and banking information. If you know your team must record that information for the sake of your downstream process or the regulations under which your business operates, then by all means, it should be required every time you are onboarding a new client. But what if your confident programmers have set your addresses up in a way that only accepts US, Canadian, or Western European addresses, and you are about to onboard your first substantial investor from South Korea? Do you want your employees to lose the benefit of everything you've invested in the system while they onboard this new customer by hand, using paper, sticky notes, and spreadsheets circulated via email? Do you want them to have to enter incorrect representations of addresses into the system because the system wouldn't allow them to bypass that control despite a valid exception? Of course not. You want to give them a way (it could be just as simple as a text field for other info) to enter nonstandard or nonconforming data while remaining inside a conforming process.

Consider the challenge of a mortgage processor working on an application from someone with no credit rating because they have no need for credit. What if a wealthy individual worth hundreds of millions of dollars wants to purchase a home for $2 million? Their financial advisor may have told them that it would make more sense to finance the house and keep their money in high-growth investments while paying a relatively low interest rate for the money borrowed for their home. A rigid system might auto-score the person, find a low credit rating due to the lack of credit experience, and decline the mortgage. Undoubtedly, central planners have already considered this and made a way for the supervisor to approve the loan, but what if the supervisor is on vacation? What will happen next is another form of workaround. As the system will not allow the process to move forward, the employee may begin to run the process offline. The largest loan working its way through a particular office is invisible now. That impacts compliance, financial forecasts, and many other critical indicators that leaders and regulators use to run or monitor an organization. There may even be legal implications. Another option, with differing negative ramifications, is that the traveling supervisor tells the employee, "Here's my password; just log in as me and make the change, and I'll change my password when I get back." Things like this happen and have very negative consequences.

These are examples of why empowering line-level contributors to handle exceptions WITHIN a system is so critical. People generally want to do great work. They want to deliver consistently. They want their customers (internal and external) to be happy with what they get. So when they run into system limitations that keep them from being able to do that, they will find a way to get things done. That is why you want your people to be able to execute traceable workarounds WITHIN your system so that their work remains visible and accountable without anyone having to share their passwords.

Let's summarize the elements required to achieve consistent delivery. They are:

- A commitment to iterative process improvement,
- A commitment to controls that ensure necessary information and artifacts are gathered at the correct times or stages within a process to reduce human errors and foreseeable exceptions,
- That changes and the impact of changes are clearly communicated, and
- Great contributors are empowered to take traceable off-ramps when they need to go around unforeseen obstacles and to grab another on-ramp to keep the process moving within the "loose-fitting but ever-tightening" systems we design and deploy.

The Auditors Are Coming! Is every industry becoming a regulated industry?

As of the writing of this book, ESG (Environmental, Social, and Governance) efforts are currently affecting many organizations that would not previously have thought of themselves as regulated companies or industries. Many organizations' ability to access credit and investment is now impacted by ESG scores (generated via external audits and scoring agencies). While this new set of regulations may or may not last, we can rest assured that something new will come along to either take its place or be added to it.

Government regulations, industry self-regulation, and outside audit requirements (such as ISO, GDPR, SOX, HIPAA, and others) have historically led regulation-heavy industries like financial services, insurance, energy, manufacturing, and government organizations to value traceability and auditing. The recent emergence of investor-led or investor-supported regulations or guidelines like ESG may now place every public and private entity under increasing scrutiny.

The impact of the metastasizing of regulation is that the rest of the world is now playing catch-up to those heavily regulated industries. Those organizations were already accustomed to addressing compliance and auditing readiness as part of their standard processes. They also understand the risks of regulatory lapses or audit failures. Not only are some organizations behind the proverbial eight-ball in process management and improvement, but they now also find themselves having to go through painful iterations of trial and error in risk management and audit readiness.

Risk arrives when things that should be audit-ready go off track. As we have already discussed, things will go off track whether or not you believe they will. That's why (at risk of overstating the point) agility is critical. Risk reduction should be a natural byproduct of standardization, process improvement, automation, and recordation. Agile process management takes that to the next level, empowering real-time risk management and mitigation. For too long, risk managers have functioned as trailing examiners of what has already happened when they should be real-time co-navigators of an operation. The old model of compliance typecast risk managers as terrified control freaks with the power to remotely pull the proverbial handbrake while the business labors to outrun aggressive competitors. In other words, it pitted them against each other. The new compliance model creates real-time visibility, enabling risk managers to act as co-navigating partners with the business. They ride along in real-time, helping the company find the best course. They can see all the transactions and exceptions happening in real-time and submit risk-mitigating course corrections as needed on the fly.

Regardless of your organization's compliance regime, you must establish visibility into the business processes at the heart of your compliance and risk management efforts. That is key to achieving and maintaining agility and speed in an increasingly regulated business world. If you cannot gain visibility into who is doing what and when in real-time, you are running blind. If you cannot see your operations, establishing appropriate real-time controls or procedures will be impossible, and your organization will struggle to pass audits.

Another concern with operating under a reactive model of regulatory management is the frequent immaturity of regimes where one system is used for doing work, and another is used to record compliance data. That is compounded when organizations lack a centralized repository for business processes because different compliance requirements are addressed using many discrete processes and platforms. When each group has their operational or compliance data stored in various places, this creates data silos that blind an organization by reducing access to the critical real-time data needed to make good decisions. That further exacerbates the risk of slowdowns from an organization's risk management and auditing efforts. Even worse, it can lead to failed audits or broken laws.

Under such circumstances, there is no single source of truth that can be relied upon, and many organizations find themselves returning to the pre-audit nightmare of working long hours in a rush to find the data required by the auditor or facing the ever-present temptation to fabricate data the night before the auditor arrives. Many auditors have shared stories with us regarding having to note that all of the entries, under various staff members' names, in a year's worth of logs appeared to have been written in the same handwriting and with the same pen. That's not what a nervous banker or investor wants to see.

In this broken model, not only is process improvement slowed down, but the interdepartmental cross-fertilization of ideas and best practices is hindered because of the creation of these compliance silos.

Once you accept that your industry is or will soon be highly regulated, selecting and implementing an agile workflow or process management platform becomes a clear imperative to address compliance and risk management in concert. A work management platform, by design, provides complete visibility into business processes and workflows in real-time. By creating and managing end-to-end business processes within a unified platform, your organization can "bake in" the compliance and risk management controls you need, regardless of the specific compliance regime you are governed by.

Embedding compliance rules and controls into the everyday workflows that your employees use to complete their work ensures that responsible staff completes the required behavior and actions. For instance, with many modern work or process management platforms, you can:

- Require the attachment of files at certain stages of a process,
- Require specific inputs before a request can enter a process or be advanced to the next stage,
- Ensure that all required information has been entered before a process can be marked as completed,
- Reopen work that meets pre-determined criteria and route it to an internal auditor or a specialized group trained to handle a particular type of risk or problem.
- Under this approach to compliance, your organization becomes more agile and responsive to changing business conditions, customer demands, and the ever-changing requirements of regulators or compliance regimes simultaneously. Significant cost savings can be gained, and reporting and auditing can be streamlined at the same time.

Deploying a unified work platform intended to address operations and compliance demands agility. Achieving this delivers unified visibility into business processes and work-flow and the transparency required for effective real-time compliance and risk management.

Some of the straightforward best practice examples we have encountered of applying agile process improvement to standard back-office work include:

- Fund management compliance and reporting, including scheduling recurring tasks and deadlines to assure regulator and customer reporting and notifications.
- Client Onboarding for Regulated Financial Services
- Insurance underwriting processes, tracking and managing risks, claims, account change requests, broker credentialing, and many other supporting tasks as they move through the underwriting, customer service, claims, and stakeholder relations processes.
- Oil and gas pipeline and utility compliance for multiple international, federal, state, county and municipal jurisdictions across thousands of separate legal agreements, covenants, and regulatory considerations.
- Stringent HR onboarding procedures in banking, including compliance with government oversight requirements.
- Environmental compliance and legal documentation for grants management, including streamlining and speeding up compliance auditing.

In addition, here are a few more in-depth examples: These represent companies that previously had manual processes. Now, they have leveraged automation to facilitate audit-ready processes, fully satisfying compliance and regulatory concerns while providing real-time reporting and visibility across the organization.

- Global Private Wealth Management: All client-facing work has been centralized. Process improvement teams have engaged more than 85% of the workforce, and their work and workflows are managed through traceable systems. Workflows manage RFPs, Cashflow,

Investments, Portfolios, Trading, Regulatory procedures and deadlines (Article 62, CTI, SRDII, etc.), Document and report generation, and evidence for internal and external audits. The standup of new business units. The development and administration of EPIs (Equity Portfolio Implementations), Data Governance, AFC (Operational Anti-Financial Crime programs), and Market Access all have workflows built to automate their work. The organization has also integrated with all key internal systems and third-party platforms (PowerBI, Cashflow Service, CRM, StatPro, and AML (Anti-Money Laundering).

- Global Investment Management Firm: Process improvement across Fund Services, Portfolio Administration, Client Transactions, Client Reporting, Client Invest Services, Operational Program Management, and HR Data Management. Projects, tasks, and workflows covering generic areas such as Project Management, Recurring Work, Incident Tracking & Reporting, Risk Assessment, Data Governance, Service & Activity Analysis, HR/ Employee Onboarding, Investment & Advisory, Outsourcing Management, Vendor Management, Audit Management, Governance, Private Deals, Capital Calls, Class Actions, Receivables Buy Out, Large Flow Oversight, Fund Launch Management, Client Lifecycle Management, Corporate Actions, Bank Loan Processing, and Counterparty Ratings.
- National Financial Services Firm: The primary focus is regulations, compliance, and auditing. Advising HFAs (Housing Finance Agencies) on how to manage cash flow as regulated by the SEC (Securities Exchange Commission) and the MSRB (Municipal Securities

Rulemaking Board). Standardized the process for providing advisory services to manage financial recommendations and operational assistance provided to HFAs throughout the US, tracking requirements and deadlines for municipal bond sale fundraising programs for clients and investors. Core workflow manages and reports on the compliance framework, review, approval, and validation steps to meet regulatory requirements.

- Private Equity Real Estate Investment Firm: Lender Reporting, Monthly Operating Reports, Quarterly Investor Reports, Recurring Templates/Tasks (Policy Renewal, Loan Maturity, Rent Rolls, etc.), Property Management, Tenant Requests & Onboarding, Moves, Adds and Changes, Preventative Maintenance Schedules and Capital Cycles, Capital Projects, Acquisitions and Due Diligence processes, Leases, Accounting Cycles, Marketing, and other operational areas.
- Global Manufacturing Company: Serving component markets in aerospace, automotive, defense, industrial, marine, mining and construction, oil and gas, power generation, and transportation and tooling. Automated upfront and estimating workflows. Sales, Customer Service, Product Management, and Finance. Credit Checks, Scope of Work Development, Specification Approvals. Forge Operations, Metallurgy Spec and Review, Purchasing, Quality Assurance to ISO standards, Procedural Library and Controls, Government Spec and Standards Compliance, Testing, Certification, etc.
- Multinational Insurance Carrier: Centralized workflows across operations managing premiums and

claims. Processes are now in place to track, manage, and report all transaction data from cover holders and service companies. Credit Control, Reconciliation, and Reporting, including multiple review, approval, and confirmation levels. Claims Recovery, Cover Holding Tracking, Query Management, Due Diligence, Compliance, Risk Assessment, Data Quality Control, Financial Reconciliation, General Procurement, Reinsurance Processes, Third Party Agreements and Administration, Contract Management, Internal Service and Support ticketing, Audit Operations, Property and Reserve Administrations, as well as direct Marine, Specialty lines, and Settlement Management, etc.

- Government DoD and Intelligence Community: Redacted (but it would be cool if we could tell you!)
- Electric Supply and Wholesale Power Contracts Management: Contract Management Process, Data Capture for/from Biomass, Fuel Cell, Nuclear, Wind, and Solar. Regulated Oversight of Contracts, Sources Development, Service Status, Output, Production, Commitments, Finances, Regulatory, Buy/Sell agreements, Legal, etc.

The Best Team Wins, How Process Helps Build the Best Teams!

In a digitally connected world, keeping the price of your product or services a secret is now an ancient memory for most industries. Likewise, it has become equally difficult for a company to keep secret its lackluster commitment to service. Consumers and B2B buyers have established federations that can now overpower the most impressive of corporate propaganda. The differences between your product and your closest competitors have become public information, especially the quality of the products and services you offer and the level of service and support you provide after the sale.

That means that while you would like to advertise your product as "best in class," your customers will now decide that. Even if you are right about the design or quality of your product, if your Customer Experience (CX) is lacking, your product may soon find itself sliding into a swamp of mediocre competitors and low margins, never to emerge again.

In this new reality, your team's commitment to never ship a defective product or quickly resolve every defect or error is paramount.

But what if the people who make our product or deliver our service hate their jobs!?

What a great question!

A compelling customer experience is nearly impossible to produce if the employees tasked with providing that experience don't like their jobs. The implementation of technology alone is not going to make an unhappy employee a good one. However, the lack of adequate technology can make good employees feel terrible about their jobs, pushing them to descend into a state where they become unhappy employees, which is awful for a business. A lack of effective processes, especially for a newly trained or poorly trained employee, can create significant challenges when something goes wrong because the employee has no idea how to resolve the problem. That can convert someone who woke up in the morning hoping to make a difference in the world into someone who looks like they don't care anymore.

I'm sure you've experienced it: you walk into a shop to report a problem with the item or service you just received. You are hoping that you are the only one with this problem, but instead, you see the employee's shoulders drop down in despair while their face says, "I'm going to apologize, but I have no idea how to resolve your problem or make you happy." You quickly realize this is not going to be a good experience.

Consider a financial services business about to onboard new funds. The excited salespeople report they've already got customers ready to subscribe. The money is burning a hole in their pockets! They meet with the person in compliance and say, "I thought we were going to have this fund live last week." Imagine their frustration when the compliance officer reports, "Sorry, there are new documents we must file because of recent legislation. There is no way for me to clear the fund for new sales because the system doesn't have a way for me to attach the new form, but it requires that I sign off stating that all required documents are attached. I'm waiting to hear back from IT." Asking a risk-averse compliance officer to work around the rules is the process equivalent of a dead end on a one-way road.

That is an example of a lack of process agility, which creates an obstacle to the smooth flow of work. The impact in this example is significant. Perhaps in the millions or tens of millions of dollars. How does that employee feel when they cannot resolve the problem? What if they go to their supervisor, and the supervisor is equally dumbfounded? What if they escalate to IT, who realizes that this part of their process will be challenging to change because the programmer who set it up just quit? Let's return to the excited salesperson with eager subscribers waiting in the wings, now worried about losing them. How do they feel about their job today?

The statement that the best team wins is intuitive, but considering what we've discussed above, the best team is not simply the team that has been recruited, paid, and trained well. Instead, the team that also has a smooth running process for delivering is the one that will win. If we take that further, we will see that a team must also be able to make changes rapidly when problems are discovered. The team must either be empowered to make changes to technical systems or to make temporary workarounds within the system while others make those changes for them. You could hire a group of Ivy League MBAs to run a customer service department. However, without that agility, you would still find them frustrated by being unable to deliver an exceptional customer experience. Imagine their shame.

We all know that Customer Experience is critical in the modern age of real-time feedback. But I hope that we have also made the case that without addressing Employee Experience (EX), achieving a winning Customer Experience may be impossible.

Some of the most critical factors that impact employee experience are:

- Communications from employers that foster trust
- Low-friction, collaborative digital work environments
- A sense of being part of a team environment
- Feeling heard and valued (training and recognition)

Let's dig into these items just a bit further:

- 'The desire for low-friction, collaborative digital work environments' is not specific to office or knowledge workers. New entrants in the workforce are increasingly digitally savvy. They have already been trained to receive instructions rapidly through a mobile device. Compliance will win them points! Enough compliance may even get them on "the leaderboard."

- What does 'Feeling heard and valued (training and meaningful recognition)' mean? One obvious conclusion we could draw is that employees want to be able to tell someone when they have hit one of those impasses that keeps them from doing great work. After all, they want to be on the leaderboard! They want to know that if something keeps them from winning at the game of work, someone will listen to them and help them solve the problem. They are already used to doing this when their downloaded app doesn't work well. Apps with great reviews are not trouble-free, but their reviews are full of comments about how surprised the user was to receive a response from the developers when they reported a problem and that the next version fixed it. Imagine if you could make your employees feel the same way when they reported an obstacle to delivering a great experience to your customers.

    o These critical, tech-savvy, best-of-breed employees want to know that they will be heard regarding where things should go and get an opportunity to get their hands on the wheel. In other words, the digitally enabled workforce of the future doesn't just want a favorable digital experience; they want to be part of improving it.

There are many factors to consider regarding employee experience. However, the case we make is that a superior employee experience is tightly connected to feedback mechanisms that foster engagement and the smooth execution of process-based contributions in a digitally accelerating world.

The best team wins! The best team uses processes to ensure they can win. The best team equips its people to help improve those processes, and the best team turns their bright young ideators into engaged stakeholders by providing them with training and opportunities to make a difference.

Encourage your organization to abandon the outdated idea that process improvement is something done as a luxury *after* achieving success. Why? Without process improvement, you may find yourself having a difficult time ever getting to that plateau. Instead, champion the idea that process improvement is necessary for your path to success and maintaining your momentum.

Growth and results are not driven by what you promise, but by what you deliver.

We previously mentioned Carl Sewell's excellent book titled *Customers for Life*. Another key takeaway from that book is in the Systems Not Smiles chapter. Sewell's premise is that customers coming into his dealership seeking service for their Cadillacs were not nearly as interested in well-dressed, smiling service writers who remembered their name and greeted them in flowery terms as most in his industry believed. They were interested in working with competent people empowered by competent systems. They wanted to interact with well-supported and well-trained service writers who noticed things like the fact that they had just had their car in the shop a week earlier. If that was true, and the problem was related, his customers wanted those service writers to confidently assure them that their unplanned return would be handled appropriately. He knew that his customers wanted service professionals to proactively contact the customer if the service would not be finished when they said it would be. The customer didn't want to call in to find out why they had not gotten their car back yet.

At the most fundamental level, Carl Sewell understood that a good process is a powerful tool and an incredible competitive advantage. He reported that high trust between his customers and service professionals increased sales. Likewise, your customer's experience will be driven more by your process than your people. Of course, you must have excellent people, but as we laid out in the previous section, two teams with exceptional people are not equal. The team with a better process will win. They will not only be empowered to deliver a better customer experience but also be more energized because they don't have to do heroic work to overcome inefficient or broken systems.

Great people empowered by great systems have more time to focus on continuously improving their processes. That is a classic example of the virtuous cycle. Your commitment to empowering your people with great tools and systems is how you deliver a great employee experience and how you empower them to deliver excellent customer experiences.

Richard and Maurice McDonald, the little-known founders of McDonalds (unless you've seen the movie *The Founder*), developed the "Speedee Service System" in the 1950s. Their process-based method revolutionized the fast-food industry. The McDonald brothers are due their honor for creating a system that so accelerated and standardized their offering that they inspired the creation of many other famous restaurant chains around the world, including household names like Taco Bell. Their revelation was that the whole roadside food industry was focused on giving customers choices when what those customers really wanted was a consistent product delivered quickly and affordably. The brothers shocked onlookers when they closed their relatively new and successful restaurant for three months to simplify their menu, standardize their processes, and rearrange the workstations for all their employees to facilitate a near-instantaneous delivery of a customer's order.

Anyone with children will know that should you ever succumb to the temptation to stop and quickly get them a McDonalds' Happy Meal, you'll find those golden arches now eliciting a fuss every time you pass another McDonalds when those children are hungry. It may even have the same effect when they are not hungry! Everyone, including the youngest consumers, knows that those arches, regardless of where you see them, represent a predictable product. If you pull into that drive-through, you know that a struggling franchise may take two minutes to deliver your food, while a smooth-running one may have your food out to you in 15 to 20 seconds. You know what a Big Mac will taste like. It might not look as good as the commercial, but it will likely taste the same from America to Japan and anywhere between.

That consistency results from the original McDonald brothers' obsession with how their processes could be standardized and orchestrated to facilitate their employees to deliver what the customer expected quickly. They had determined how process could be employed to make their employees' jobs easier and their customers' expectations easier to meet. The result was that McDonalds soon became one of the most successful franchises in history.

If your work management ecosystem is a back office operation like a financial services company, you may ask yourself, "Are the authors suggesting we should model our business after McDonalds?" No, and yes. You run a far more complex and necessarily customized operation, but in the end, significant aspects of what you do *can* be preconfigured, automated, or streamlined to help achieve similarly consistent and predictable outcomes.

What we can all glean from McDonalds is this: If you are willing to hyper-focus on how your work is arranged, the decisions your employees must make along the way, and precisely what they need to have at their fingertips to get the job done, and avoid the potential for unexpected or negative variations in outcomes, you too will have the opportunity to briefly slow down in the short-term to facilitate a massive acceleration of your organization across time.

One of the organizations we (HighGear) worked with during the early development of our software was a 100-year-old furniture factory. They sold high-end furniture designed in Italy and constructed in the United States. When the business and their cross-Atlantic relationships were first established, the cost of materials and labor was far more competitive in the United States. The items built here were shipped back to Europe and sold as "Italian furniture." Over the more than one hundred years that ensued, the market changed quite a bit. Their European connections were still meaningful, and some of the furniture was still sold in Europe. However, their current primary sales market was now in the United States. They were beginning to feel competitive pressures because while they were experts at the physical process of building furniture, they had fallen behind in the digital realm of their business.

Their physical processes were impressive. While the building they worked in felt like a throwback to another era, their commitment to process improvement in that physical realm was cutting-edge. To give an example of just how advanced they were in the realm, let's quickly delve into a term we first encountered in that engagement: MODAPTS.

MODAPTS stands for the Modular Arrangement of Predetermined Time Standards. MODAPTS uses a "time studies" technique to record, break down, and encode manual labor into individual repeatable modular steps. This organization had indeed taken that effort to the extreme. For example, if a worker was going to connect two dovetailed pieces of wood, the organization had separate coded steps to cover how long it took to dispense the glue onto each side of the part. The time required to set the glue bottle back down with the cap tightened was also known. If the parts were going to be clamped and set aside, every step in that routine was independently measured. Therefore, if a new furniture design required eight parts to be glued together, their "work engineers" could associate the individual codes for the labor steps and quickly assemble a nearly perfect prediction of the time required to complete the assembly.

However, their systems for tracking these precisely modeled steps were all managed on paper. Changing a MODAPTS time element (for instance, if a new tool had been developed that cut a step's time in half) would require hunting down the folder with the spec for that MODAPTS element and changing it there. It also meant that the work instructions for every "furniture recipe" flowing across the organization that used that step now also needed to be found and modified.

That case study exemplifies an excellent system with extremely low agility. The competitive pressures they faced in the market forced them to revamp their product offerings quickly and radically. However, the complexity of making those changes had now become their Achilles' heel.

Unfortunately, the effort required to take their massive legacy of work and put it into any state-of-the-art digital system was just too high. Due to market pressure from more agile competitors, they already faced significant financial difficulties.

Sadly, less than nine months later, this company, which had survived for over a century, closed its doors. This example is shared to underscore an important point. Process improvement alone is not enough because markets change, requirements change, and expectations change. The configuration of organizations also changes over time, even if their products or services remain unchanged. For instance, mergers and acquisitions often cause teams with similar functions to merge or rearrange their duties to avoid duplication. Well-implemented processes are a significant advantage for the teams that wield them, but if those processes are brittle or difficult to change, they can quickly become a disadvantage. Rigid processes can eventually slow down a market-leading organization while newer or more nimble competitors rapidly adapt to changing environments. That is why it is critical to ensure that the systems you implement facilitate your competitive advantage and are flexible enough to keep pace with the one constant you can always count on: Change.

You cannot control the market, but can control your ability to adapt to it.

Your process experts can determine why your front-line or back-office employees encounter new difficulties. However, they will never be able to ascertain root causes as quickly as those front-line or back-office employees themselves. That is why Lean Manufacturing advocates use the term 'going to the Gemba.' They want to go where the deed was done to find the problem. If the process-minded contributors across your organization can quickly and effectively implement work-arounds or minor changes within your systems, you will have empowered them to keep work flowing. You will also have developed insights into whether more extensive changes are required. It may be time to bring in the process experts. But your work is not stuck or running 'off book' while your new requirements are being ascertained and planned.

Facilitating that level of agility will require thinking and systems that deliberately support delegated administration. Delegated administration is a concept whereby processes and the automation that supports them get segmented into modular components where:

There are clear departmental (or functional) inputs and outputs (e.g., "We send the document to legal to review. Once they approve it and add their disclaimers, it goes to our publishing team.").

- Localized autonomy makes sense (e.g., "Bob decides who will work on what legal approvals and is aware of all their requirements").
- Local resources have been trained (i.e., administrators can safely change elements of those components).
- Guidelines, protocols, or technical controls are implemented to ensure that any changes cannot have unintended consequences elsewhere within a process.

At a basic level, imagine one of Carl Sewell's service writers noticing a mechanic struggling to find the right car in a parking lot as their dealership grows. The original method was to record the automobile's license plate number on the work order handed to the mechanic. That may have worked fine when there were only 10 or 12 cars in a straight line, but once there are three rows of cars in a service lot, the license plates on the rear rows of cars would no longer be visible. A savvy service writer may quickly decide to write that same license plate number on large hang tags and hang them from the cars' rearview mirrors where they are more easily seen. Problem solved!

By enabling a straightforward workaround at the local level (permission for simple improvements should not be required), something that previously cost valuable time can quickly be solved. The question is, how do you ensure that this process doesn't break down or encounter unexpected outcomes elsewhere?

Feedback mechanisms are the answer.

In this baseline process example solved with a simple hangtag, this small change is unlikely to cause challenges elsewhere in the business. However, if someone changes the format of the numbering on those tags later, the implications could become more complex. Thus, the means, scope, and timeliness of change-related communications will also become more important. However, the need for clear communication doesn't justify removing the ability to solve problems at the level where the problem exists.

Organizations considering process as an advantage must also begin working to develop these and other change-related disciplines. We will elaborate on these further and provide various best practice examples in Part 3.

Remember, process improvement aims to deliver more consistent and streamlined customer outcomes. It doesn't matter whether your customer is the next team in a multi-departmental process or the end user of your company's product or offering. Your goal remains the same. You're trying to facilitate your team's ability to deliver that consistent outcome quickly. That is where your business is likely very different than McDonalds. Their limited number of well-tested menu items makes adaptation relatively uncommon. Still, as a bit of trivia, even McDonalds offers a veggie burger in at least one location in a vegetarian market in India. That's an example of macro standards being effectively intertwined with local flexibility.

When change in your marketplace is a constant, your business or organization's ability to adapt to that change must also be a constant if you are to remain competitive.

So, in conclusion, having great people is a must for any organization that wants to excel. Empowering those people with processes that make it easy to deliver consistency is also necessary for any organization that wants to keep those people. And finally, ensuring that those systems leave them the flexibility required to adapt to change quickly is vital to maintaining competitive advantage across time.

Takeaways

- People want to be seen as problem solvers and contributors by the people around them.
- Systems need to help employees solve problems within those systems and should never force them to create external workarounds.
- If you empower people to build and improve processes dynamically, they will own their processes and want to prove how well they work. That will attract other people who want to be part of an excellent team. That is a virtuous cycle that organizations can leverage.
- Organizations that want process to be an advantage will invest in:
  - How an organization's work is arranged,
  - The decisions that must be made along the way and exactly what those contributors need to have at their fingertips (decision support) to make them quickly while avoiding the potential for unexpected or negative variations in outcomes,

---

o Providing the framework, governance, and EMPOWERMENT for their A+ team players. The winning subsystems that team members long to create, manage, and continuously improve will be the process-savvy organization's 'process dividend.'

· Committed process champions willing to stop and invest in process improvement in the short term will facilitate substantial ROI through acceleration for their organizations over time.

PART TWO

THE EMPIRE BUILDER'S DILEMMA

CHAPTER THREE

THE PROBLEM WITH ATTEMPTING TO CHANGE EVERYTHING BEFORE CHANGING ANYTHING

We've all experienced it: An organization you've worked with has given you a consistent experience over time, but now they have implemented a new system. You can hear their customer service representatives using broken speech to shield their confusion as it escalates into frustration. It sounds something like, "That's odd! Huh. I would've thought… That's weird! Maybe it will be on this other screen. Can you hold on for a couple of minutes? Let me get my supervisor to look at this with me." When they return five or six minutes later, they apologize and halfheartedly report that they sorted it all out. With a seemingly disingenuous positive tone, they tell you, "We just put a new system in, and there was no place for us to put that information in for you, but I've put some notes into your account, and my supervisor has promised she is going to look into it later. Don't worry; we'll take care of this for you." Because you trust the organization, you may take their advice and decide not to worry. Perhaps you should.

Even if they can sort out your issue (but often they don't unless you remind them), their cost structure is still going up significantly. Perhaps it will appear in one of your future bills as they raise their prices to cover the costs of this new 'stream-lined way of doing business.' Or perhaps they won't be in business any longer at all. They may even have to sell to one of their larger competitors. All these things could lead to a rough ride for you as their consumer. Consider what's happening behind the scenes:

- The bewildered employee who couldn't figure out where to put your change of information has lost several minutes and perhaps missed a performance metric. They also felt foolish when you heard them struggling to do their job.
- They put you on hold for several minutes. Their phone system may soon need an upgrade to handle the increased number of connected people at any given time because they are not the only people dealing with unhandled exceptions.
- The supervisor who was hoping to meet with IT to explain the many challenges with the new systems has a long line of people waiting at her desk instead. They are all seeking help with problems like the one your customer service rep is waiting to bring to her attention.
- Not only is that supervisor feeling overwhelmed, but she can't figure the problem out, even with her higher privileges in the new system. She sends her disheart-ened and previously productive customer service rep back to tell you they are putting notes in the system. They are both worried your record will get lost until you call in again to complain.
- Instead of typing an address in a field, your rep must now type several sentences of notes to ensure that when

someone else reads this a few days, weeks, or months from now, they won't think she failed to do her job.

- A simple change like this used to take moments and allowed the rep to use the rest of her time to have a delightful and confidence-inspiring conversation with you. She would also have told you about the company's latest promotion and your opportunity to upgrade. Instead, trust has now been eroded. This call has now taken 10 minutes, left you wondering if your new address will get recorded correctly, and left your rep wondering if it will be okay. The supervisor now wonders if it's time to get her resume together.
- You were not offered that upgrade. There was no chance to increase their revenue based on your long history and confidence in this company you do business with.
- When you call a month or two later to ask why your account change wasn't made as requested and promised, you discover that the rep you worked with has left. The supervisor to whom your simple change had been escalated has also gone. The new employee will assure you that they will take care of it and take more notes to address the change they are not empowered to make.
- You are now an at-risk customer who would consider switching to a competitor.

With a few specifics changed, almost every reader of this book can likely think of a recent interaction with an organization that delivered a similar lackluster experience. It may be an insurance company you previously trusted, but now it doesn't seem to have their act together. It may be a cell phone provider that can't seem to find your account – though they manage to bill your card each month. It might be a trusted law firm or an investment advisor who's recently merged with another company and is in the middle of changing systems. The net of it is this: someone made a big plan that didn't include the little details, and you are experiencing the impacts.

Many leaders believe they can single-handedly ascertain everything their organization needs and successfully introduce their new and better plan and system all at once. Some will succeed, but, by far, most will not.

"When organizations undertake a transformation to improve performance, research shows those efforts fail 70 percent of the time." [8]

Some will claim to have succeeded. Those leaders will do this using a sliding scale and a long time window. They ignore that an honest assessment would show that the organization experienced high stress levels, reduced morale, and employee turnover before their "great results" emerged. Leaders often wind up too busy trying to prove their success to realize or count the lost time, heavy consulting fees, or reputations and relationships damaged along the way.

The new system claimed it would address all the organization's challenges in one fell swoop. How wonderful! Our brave new world is on the way! We no longer need to wield all those spreadsheets or deal with our old manually-rigged systems (A.K.A workarounds)! These kinds of fantasies are exciting and the stuff that corporate visions are often littered with, but they are rarely accurate. While these new systems are big and impressive from that perspective, their all-at-once implementations are frequently referred to within the process improvement vernacular as a "Big Bang."

---

[8] https://www.mckinsey.com/capabilities/rts/our-insights/mind-sets-matter-in-transformations-a-conversation-with-jon-garcia

> Workarounds are the organic micro-processes that people implement when systems don't provide a means for keeping work moving forward at various block points.

When these systems are rolled out, any fatal flaw (or missed workaround) that went unnoticed during discovery is suddenly on full display when the flaw becomes a dead end or blockade. These discoveries continue as varied workflows through the new and often brittle architecture. Workers who used to depend on the decision support provided by these micro-organically developed workarounds now find that the new system has paved them over. Frustration quickly mounts, tensions grow, and customers may not understand, but they can feel the impact. Morale declines, turnover begins, and the already busy leaders start working to fix the "big bang" and quickly become overwhelmed.

At HighGear, we sometimes use the metaphor of a big robot. The business comes to IT with a concept in mind. They want big automation! They have envisioned a big, friendly robot that will carry them along and make them look like heroes as they get their customers' work done more quickly. The IT department gets excited, too! They have been waiting for somebody to come along and fund their idea for a giant robot. It's going to be great!

The problem is they don't quite have the same vision. While the business has pictured C3PO, the mild-mannered and friendly droid of Star Wars fame, IT has been picturing a hundred-foot-tall battle droid! The difference is never quite that obvious but becomes glaringly apparent once the robot is delivered.

When the business unit's "big new automation" finally arrives, they are shocked to see that the giant robot has no heart and no brain, and everyone who interacts with it can see some part of the problem.

We say that it *has no brain* because the selection or design of the system was completed without the detailed input of stakeholders closest to the problem. Thus, the organizational knowledge hidden away in those workarounds has all been lost.

We say that *it has no heart* because the people using the system don't support the new system. After all, for some, it's not what they asked for, and for others, they never asked for this change in the first place. And without an organic commitment to a successful change, the finger-pointing and blame cycles begin.

User adoption, which we will discuss in more detail in *Chapter 5, Background III*, is critical to the success of any new process or system. Without it, your new launch will fail. Some will claim success after replacing most of the users. But is that a success?

Can big organizations survive this kind of turnover of staff and customers? Yes, they can and frequently do. However, it often becomes the vulnerability in their armor or the spot where newer, faster, and more agile competitors can attack to leverage the moment and find their opportunity.

The Apollo Missions and Process Emergence

Before we break down and analyze the differences between the traditional methods and the newer more agile (emergent) model for process improvement and change management, we will take a reasonably concise but critical detour. This true story is a perfect larger-than-life example of how high-stakes workarounds made the difference between life and death for a small group of astronauts. We share this metaphor and our analysis to help highlight the power and process of bricolage and the critical motivations and operational necessities that lead to the vital workarounds we find keeping every organization running, whether their management knows it or not. Our team presented this story as an example of bricolage at one of our past customer conferences, and it received very positive feedback. We asked Matthew Rodatus, one of HighGear's Senior Software Engineers, to pull the story behind that presentation into the following narrative. It serves as a metaphor for the concepts behind how workarounds are developed and the criticality of identifying, understanding, and ultimately valuing them as a core component of any successful change or transformation effort.

> Bricolage can be defined as an item or solution put together using whatever happens to be within reach or available at the time a need arises.

Nothing held the US public's attention like the Apollo missions. Starting with President Kennedy's challenge in 1961 to land a man on the moon, with a safe return to Earth, by the end of the decade, the US was mesmerized as our country achieved what appeared to be that period's most remarkable feat of human ingenuity and remains one of the singular achievements of the last hundred years. Building on the foundation of Project Mercury and Project Gemini, the Apollo missions were destined to propel our ambition out of low Earth orbit all the way to the surface of the moon. But not first without failure and tragedy.

A fire in the command module during a launch pad test on January 27, 1967, resulted in the failure of the Apollo 1 mission and the tragic deaths of Gus Grissom, Ed White, and Roger B. Chaffee. An Accident Review Board quickly determined the technical cause of the fire. They found that it was due to a combination of an electrical problem and various flammable attributes of the command module, such as the high-oxygen environment. The serious problems found were enough to suspend crewed Apollo flights for almost two years until these issues could be resolved.

The principal issue, however, was a failure of process. Human insight and ingenuity are vital to advancing human knowledge and achievement and the power driving miraculous rescues when crises occur. However, the Apollo missions began without a thoroughness of lessons learned in earlier missions and experiments and lacked a sober awareness of the complexity and risks of lunar travel. Complex endeavors such as this require learned experience to be converted into repeatable processes that can be executed effectively (and safely) even when there are human errors. That is the idea of process emergence, the genesis of a new process that encompasses and yet transcends the process it started as. Awareness of this phenomenon is essential in applications where process failure has a high impact, such as when human life is at stake.

The Saturn IB AS-204, the rocket to be launched into low Earth orbit for the Apollo 1 mission, was unfueled during the launchpad test on January 27. The absence of fuel was assumed to present a lower risk to the astronauts' lives, and therefore, sufficient emergency precautions were neglected. However, due to the internal pressure of the cabin, the hatch could not be opened during the rescue attempt.

If the escape procedures had been thoroughly tested, these three astronauts – who all had wives and children – would have survived the launchpad test. Furthermore, these mistakes were inexcusable, given lessons already learned from prior tests.

In 1962, while testing a Gemini spacesuit in a pure oxygen chamber, a fire ignited, and Colonel B. Dean Smith and his colleague barely escaped in time. That was followed by multiple other tests involving high oxygen environments and accidents due to hardware issues with the Apollo Environmental Control System between 1964 and 1966.

Further compounding and confirming the lack of coordination and haphazardness of many space research agencies at this time, a mere four days after the Apollo 1 fire, two air personnel were trapped in a space environment simulator (again, a high oxygen environment) tending rabbits when flames ignited due to an electrical spark and perished.

Why had the various space research labs and agencies, most of all NASA, not learned from these mistakes? They had plenty of evidence (and warnings) that a high oxygen environment coupled with bad electrical wiring was a lethal recipe. Additionally, due to the multiple fatalities and close calls, the importance of escape procedures should have been evident.

However, while the Apollo missions began with failure and tragedy, they also contained tremendous human ingenuity and ultimate success with Apollo 11, the first mission to land humans on the moon. That was followed by five more missions, for a total of six, that reached the moon's surface and established the Apollo Program as one of the all-time great achievements of the nation. In addition to acquiring valuable research data and furthering scientific inquiry, such as allowing us to confirm that the moon's composition matches that of the earth, the Apollo missions galvanized the human spirit of the nation and accelerated the technology revolution, including the development of the modern computer.

With two successful lunar landings under its belt, NASA planned to continue and expand exploration of the moon with Apollo 13, with the Latin motto for the mission being *Ex luna, scientia*. While the prior missions had focused on the primary goals of attaining the moon's surface in Apollo 11 and performing a "precision landing" in Apollo 12, the next mission was to extend into more scientific observation and data gathering, most notably geology. However, as fate would have it, this mission would be hindered by an unexpected crisis that would unleash one of the most inspiring achievements of human ingenuity.

More than 80% through the journey from the Earth to the moon, the flight controller responsible for the Command and Service Module (CSM) instructed the crew to initiate a stirring of one of the oxygen tanks. (Without stirring, the contents of the tanks stratify or become less uniform, which affects the accuracy of pressure readings. Stirring re-mixes the contents and makes them more uniform so that accurate pressure readings can be obtained.) Jack Swigert, the command module pilot, performed the stirring as directed.

One and a half minutes after the stirring, the astronauts reported hearing a large bang and the unplanned firing of a set of thrusters. Upon looking outside the capsule, Commander Jim Lovell observed gas venting into space, confirming the dire reality of the situation. One of the oxygen tanks had ruptured, and two of the three fuel cells were dead. The remaining main oxygen tank was almost empty, leaving only it and the buffer oxygen tank, whose purpose was to ensure consistent pressure in the system. Once these tanks were expended, there would be no more oxygen for the command module; the third and final fuel cell would fail, resulting in a total loss of power.

The astronauts were directed to use the lunar module as a lifeboat because it still had power and oxygen. Fortunately, this is a moment where the outcome of the story differs from the Apollo 1 disaster. NASA had considered the potential of using the lunar module as a lifeboat in case of disaster, even though such an eventuality was deemed very remote. Nonetheless, as such, this emergency procedure was part of the process understood by NASA, which enabled its quick activation and ensured the immediate survival of the astronauts. That gave everyone time to tackle the next priority – returning the astronauts safely to Earth.

At the time, the spacecraft was still on a trajectory that would put it into lunar orbit to allow the detachment, touchdown, and return of the lunar module. Now, it needed to be placed on a path to swing around the moon and return to Earth, but there were two problems. The lunar module's propulsion system did not have the necessary computer instructions to control it from the lunar module, where the astronauts had emigrated to preserve the command module's limited resources, which would be needed later in the return journey. Furthermore, the debris surrounding the spacecraft and the light from the sun glinting off it hindered attempts to navigate using the surrounding stars. That was necessary to achieve an accurate maneuver.

Jim Lovell, the mission commander, who had flown space missions since Gemini 7 in 1964, fortunately had experience performing manual maneuvers under pressure. During the Apollo 8 mission, where he functioned as the command module pilot, he had already gained the experience to surmount this challenge.

The Apollo 8 mission aimed to orbit around the moon and return to Earth. It was the next step in NASA's testing of their systems and processes, each mission progressing closer and closer to the lunar surface. During some free time on the mission, Lovell was rotating the module to plot the position of stars. While using the computer keyboard, he input the wrong instructions and accidentally corrupted some of the computer memory. That caused the spacecraft's Inertial Measurement Unit (IMU) to think it was in the wrong orientation. It automatically fired thrusters to self-correct.

Under this pressure, Jim Lovell needed to perform manual calculations using the stars Rigel and Sirius, re-align the spacecraft, and input the correct data into the computer. The procedure was successful and not considered anything more than a hiccup, except that Jim Lovell gained valuable experience through it. As would occur later, what happened here almost exactly mirrored the situation on Apollo 13, where the IMU was shut down to conserve energy, and manual calculations would need to be performed in even more dire circumstances.

Because of the debris from the explosion of the oxygen tank surrounding Apollo 13, Lovell would need to perform the necessary manual calculations based on the position of the sun, which was the only star not occluded. Despite being more complex and under pressure, he successfully performed the maneuver and placed the spacecraft on a return journey. His prior experience proved critical to the safe return of the crew.

The next problem, however, was the most difficult yet. Even though the lunar module had oxygen to support the astronauts for the return journey, the carbon dioxide they were continuously exhaling needed to be removed from the cabin so that astronauts would not suffocate.

Both the command module and the lunar module had carbon dioxide scrubbers with replaceable canister filters, but there were two problems: the lunar module did not have enough canisters for the return journey to Earth, which was much longer than the duration of the lunar landing, and the canisters were incompatible between the modules.

The NASA engineers on the ground had improvised a "mailbox" solution, which would adapt the command module's canisters for use in the lunar module's carbon dioxide scrubber, using only the materials available onboard. Using the instructions from the ground, the astronauts built the device, and the carbon dioxide levels quickly returned to safe levels. In Apollo Expeditions to the Moon, a book about NASA history, Jim Lovell stated that this creation of the cartridge adapter was "a fine example of cooperation between ground and space."

That was the last serious problem in the return journey, and almost six days after launch, the crew members of Apollo 13 all returned safely home, landing in the South Pacific Ocean and being recovered by the USS Iwo Jima.

In the movie Apollo 13, based on the book written by Jim Lovell and Jeffrey Kluger, the real Jim Lovell appears in a cameo as the captain of the USS Iwo Jima, where he shakes Tom Hanks's hand, who plays Lovell in the movie.

NASA and other space research agencies learned many lessons during the early space programs. The disaster of Apollo 1 gave them a crucial awareness of the risks of high oxygen environments and bad electrical wiring, prompting a redesign of the module and the addition of more emergency precautions. The "successful failure" of Apollo 13 also prompted changes, such as redesigning the oxygen tanks so they would not require stirring fans and adding emergency water and batteries to the command module.

However, the most important lesson was about process emergence. Throughout the space program, issues occurred (sometimes repeatedly) that demanded that solutions or workarounds be added to the process for lunar travel, such as the core need for improved engineering of the electrical systems. These new scenarios bolstered the process for future success. However, in Apollo 13, the successful outcome came about by *both* the experience inherent to the existing process *and* the innovation of new situations, such as the bricolage – the construction of something out of the assortment of available materials – of the cartridge adapter for the carbon dioxide scrubber.

While the prior experience served as an excellent baseline to chart the initial course for the Apollo program, there was much knowledge gained by the boots on the ground, and numerous course corrections were needed until the process for lunar exploration was safe for human life and reliable in achieving the goal.

The human ingenuity of Apollo 13 was barely short of miraculous, but it was more than merely inspiring; it had a lesson, too. Humans need processes so that the people executing critical endeavors do not rely solely on their human competence. However, processes also require the flexibility to incorporate real-time human insights. Those creative, on-the-fly innovations and insights can surmount new and unexpected obstacles and bolster the process to transcend what is possible, given the limitations of prior knowledge. The Apollo astronauts had deep experience in the systems, processes, and challenges they encountered. In careful collaboration with NASA leadership, they were best equipped to improve the process of space travel and lunar exploration for generations to come.

References:

https://themarsgeneration.org/how-creativity-saved-the-crew-of-apollo-13/
https://en.wikipedia.org/wiki/Apollo_13
https://en.wikipedia.org/wiki/Apollo_program
https://en.wikipedia.org/wiki/List_of_Apollo_missions
https://en.wikipedia.org/wiki/Apollo_1
https://en.wikipedia.org/wiki/Gus_Grissom
https://en.wikipedia.org/wiki/Ed_White_(astronaut)
https://en.wikipedia.org/wiki/Roger_B._Chaffee
https://space.stackexchange.com/questions/2500/why-did-apollo-mission-numbering-skip-2-3-4-5-and-6
https://curator.jsc.nasa.gov/education/_documents/what%20we've%20learned%20about%20the%20moon.pdf
https://www.nasa.gov/specials/60counting/spaceflight.html
https://en.wikipedia.org/wiki/Jim_Lovell
Book: Lovell, J., & Kluger, J. (2006). Apollo 13. Houghton Mifflin (Trade).
https://en.wikipedia.org/wiki/Apollo_8
https://ntrs.nasa.gov/api/citations/19760005868/downloads/19760005868.pdf

The Big Bang and The Big Boom: Why Big Change is So Dangerous

Consider someone in an automotive assembly line discovering a particular panel frequently doesn't fit well, requiring a brief stoppage of the entire line. A worker must run to get a replacement panel each time it occurs. That is a problem worth reporting. It is also a problem worth investigating. Stopping an automotive line can cost millions of dollars per minute. Divide that minute by 60, and you realize that every time you have that problem, you are in the realm of many thousands of dollars per second. Good production engineers would want to determine the root cause of the poor panel fit to see if they could move upstream to where the panel is being produced and resolve the problem there. In the short term, they might also want to see if a simple workaround could be implemented as either an interim or permanent solution.

But what if the engineer suggests replacing the entire assembly line? What if the frustration with the constant challenges of keeping the assembly line moving has led the engineer to conclude that the entire system is flawed, should be scrapped, and built again from scratch by a new and better vendor? Would this seem like an appropriate solution for an otherwise adequately performing assembly line?

Even if we assume there *are* systemic problems, and a new assembly line might be a worthwhile investment, wouldn't it still make more sense to address the specific issues on the current line while working on an overall plan for a new one?

What would the cost be to replace an entire assembly line? What new risks would be introduced? How many production problems already resolved through workarounds might become "lost knowledge" until those same problems are reencountered on the new assembly line?

The existence of engineered and organic workarounds within our organizations proves that people are already inherently functioning as natural process improvers. This ever-present reality reinforces why we should learn to engage our organization's subject matter experts when designing new solutions. We should also remember they live where the work is done, not in the ivory towers above. This truth also reinforces the idea that we should engage and train our stakeholders to empower their contributions to our ongoing incremental process improvements – but to now do so *within* our systems as engaged stakeholders.

From time to time, automotive companies will need to build new assembly lines to incorporate new technologies such as robotics, laser-based precision welding, or changes to the component-level pre-assemblies. A radical shift in the core product design may warrant that new assembly line. However, within the lifecycle of an existing automobile model or chassis platform, it almost always makes more sense to incrementally improve the line or address unforeseen deficits or issues as problems arise. Of course, it makes more sense to improve incrementally! But this isn't just true for automotive companies.

Enterprise Resource Planning software is a class of comprehensive applications that typically provide accounting capabilities and manage the inputs and outputs necessary to run the supply chain for an entire organization. Initially focused on manufacturing and distribution organizations, ERPs typically function across verticals and serve larger organizations, from the production of items to the general ledger functions.

Consider the financial services organization that discovers they have a problem onboarding new clients because of limitations with record formatting inside their current ERP (Enterprise Resource Planning software). That would certainly be a problem worthy of reporting and investigating. After all, if a financial services organization can't onboard their clients, they can't begin charging their fees! In contrast to the assembly line example above, you might be astounded to find out how many of these financial services organizations will determine that a limitation in record formatting within an ERP is a valid reason to begin the cumbersome and often years-long process of selecting, procuring, and implementing a new ERP. So, avoid the big bang. Don't use a nuke for a gnat. Be agile and make small changes – needed changes along the way.

That's the point… and before you go there, let's first be sure you've considered what could be hidden away in that old system that might get overlooked if you head towards something new too quickly.

Why you need to know about workarounds

A growing list of workarounds could be perceived as proof that a system is not meeting the organization's needs, but that may overlook the fact that all successful systems are a combination of planned capabilities and successfully implemented workarounds. The plan that does not account for workarounds will fail because they are a part of the reality of getting systems into production and getting them adopted. Modern agile systems are, therefore, being increasingly called upon to incorporate workarounds. However, few are answering the call.

As system agility increases, the rapid inclusion of workarounds, system adoption, and system effectiveness are all improving. However, harnessing this possibility requires an up-front commitment to buying or building more agile systems. The emphasis must be on agile versus just more 'modern' systems.

Whether agility is provided through the flexibility of the system or the creativity of the human resources analyzing and implementing change, user communities determined to get their jobs done will deploy workarounds as soon as your new system is rolled out. The power of agile systems is to facilitate those workarounds *within* your new system versus in parallel.

Let's go back to our example. Your IT department says, "You are right. We cannot put client records into the ERP. We must stop and procure a new ERP." If IT stops there, your diligent and noble users, determined to onboard their new clients, will quickly pull out their trusty old spreadsheets, rogue databases, or other workarounds. They are going to get the job done!

Let the internal political battles begin. The business wants to get the job done. IT wants to make sure they do it correctly and don't expose the organization to cyber risks. Secretly, the business just wishes IT would try to fix the problem. The vendor may have told them it is possible by simply installing a new version of the software. Secretly, IT wishes the business would stop changing its mind about what is most important and let them introduce some cool technology that could solve all of these problems at the same time. They are both right, and they are both wrong. Implementing low-security workarounds can really be a significant risk to the business, but so can wholesale changes to large-scale working processes.

As an example, one of the workarounds we have seen was a business that kept new client records in a spreadsheet. The row number for the new client record (i.e., their row in the client spreadsheet) was entered into the ERP in an unused "house number" field for each client. Inside the ERP, the organization had a growing number of customers with the same name, and the only difference between them was their "house number." No one in IT noticed that for quite a while. The business was happy. They had gotten away with their workaround and had all the data they needed in their spreadsheet!

However, when a former client was deleted from the spreadsheet, all the row numbers moved. Uh-Oh! After a few days of frustration, a new workaround was required. Any row number higher than 3000 would require the ERP user to deduct one from the number so that the right record could be located in the spreadsheet. The alternative would have been to ask IT to write a script to reduce the house number by one for all the other new clients. But that would require revealing the secret workaround.

Some readers may be asking: "Why not figure out how to get the current ERP to store the records the way you want?"

In some organizations IT must legitimately rule out many available solutions. For instance, financial services firms have serious security requirements that must be addressed, as well as a variety of compliance and legal requirements that must be imposed on any viable software vendor. This reduces the field of options. Requirements for a new ERP, detailed by the business, included everything that they had learned and everything they knew they would need to record. They also detailed all the ways that information had already moved around the organization through the existing ERP. They had also diligently tried to document all their legacy workarounds to ensure the new solution would address all of them. However, as the team began to compare the viable options, they realized some of the potential systems would come with limitations that would require net new workarounds. This would be the tradeoff for being able to address shortfalls of the prior package. "That's okay! We'll just get the vendor to propose including those in the implementation phase!" And those are the famous last words of many a late and over-budget project.

One of the main purposes of this book is to take a realistic look at how things could be done differently. Let's explore the worst-case scenario: the Big Bang.

The Big Bang!

While modern systems are impressive with their comprehensive capabilities, their typical form of implementation is often referred to as "Big Bang." The Creator of the universe may have been able to pre-plan and orchestrate the arrangement of all matter, unveiling it onto the scene in just a handful of days, with it all coming together just as it was planned, but humans are rarely able to do the same thing regardless of a project's size or the number of resources assigned to it. Something usually gets missed, and the result is that our 'Big Bangs' often come off with a bit more of a big boom!

As we have already emphasized, but it is worth repeating in summary form: Many creative leaders go down the path of confident belief, convinced they can analyze and ascertain all the organization's needs in one fell swoop, then implement their new and improved systems all-at-once. However, very few succeed. Some will claim to have succeeded across the arc of time, but an honest assessment typically shows that during this kind of radical change, the organization experiences high levels of stress that lead to employee turnover, reduced morale, lower productivity, and customer frustration or loss.

I am reminded of a story (the truth of which I have not verified) of a naval vessel being produced in a small branch of the Chesapeake Bay in Virginia during wartime. The relatively large ship was constructed at the end of a comparatively small creek. This new facility was rapidly thrown together to meet the needs of wartime production. There was a great deal of concern about the size of the ship and being able to get it launched into this creek, out to the bay, and ultimately to the ocean. The engineers were sure that if they launched it at the peak of high tide, everything would be fine. The engineers had measured and calculated, and the Admirals had placed their bets. They were confident it would work. However, there were others concerned the ship could potentially run aground, and their reputations were at stake.

When this ship was ready for launch, the boat slid down off the rails at the peak of high tide in the narrow creek. It began digging up the mud as it slid into the water, making it far enough into the water to level out to where the propellers were only slightly touching the upper edges of the very soft mud. With a gentle application of the motors and careful management of the rudder, the ship was taken out into the Chesapeake Bay to great applause and reports of success.

The story I was told included this additional perspective. The Navy was sued by more than a dozen homeowners on each side of the creek who had a six-foot wall of water wash through their homes. Several small pets washed away. Some automobiles were damaged beyond repair, and a local park was nearly destroyed. Why did this happen? The answer is simple. As everyone obsessed about the perfection of their deployment, no one had stopped to consider the impact on those who were about to be affected by the change. But isn't this just a metaphor for us as we consider corporate change?

In our simple anecdote, the project was hailed as a success despite the adverse outcomes. But don't we see the same thing when people are convinced their project was a success in our modern corporate settings as well? Sometimes, the things we've overlooked are only remembered until everyone who can remember them is gone.

The people most frustrated by the experience of a challenging software rollout often give up and find employment elsewhere. Thus, the person responsible for the new rollout can soon rewrite history and tell everyone of their amazing success. Worse yet, they proclaim this past 'success' as they interview for a new position at your company, where they plan to soon repeat it!

We have seen proof that these kinds of unintended or negative outcomes can be avoided through stakeholder engagement and planned agility. We have observed clients with teams ranging from tens to tens of thousands. We have served organizations across the globe. We have seen sophisticated practitioners struggle and others elegantly succeed with change and process improvement efforts. We have studied the techniques and measured the differing results. We have developed empirically rooted and deeply held opinions on how organizations can improve the outcome and the experience of organizational change and process improvement.

In the next chapter, we will begin to share how change can be implemented in a more incremental and organic way.

CHAPTER FOUR

EMERGENCE: THE NATURAL PATTERNS OF PROCESS

"Emergence can be defined as the arising of novel and coherent structures, patterns, and properties during the process of self-organization in complex systems."
—Economist Jeff Goldstein, *Journal Emergence*

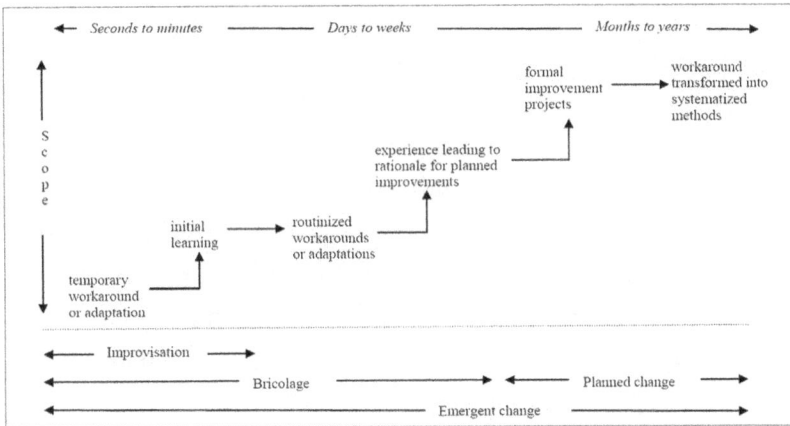

So far, we have made the case that all organizations have processes. In this chapter, we will focus on those processes that arise organically through the pattern defined in the book's opening under the definition of "emergence."

The process of natural emergence, when it is harnessed, can also be viewed as a methodical alternative to big bang planning and deployment. It is the domain of the patient tinkerer who plods towards perfection in incremental steps. With each iterative improvement, the flywheel spins just a bit faster. An emergent change is a small workaround or adaptation in the performance or flow of work because of need or opportunity.

As an organization moves through twenty years, adds a few hundred or perhaps thousands of people, maybe even an acquisition or three, it will have become that impressive coral reef that can be seen in aerial photos (i.e., an impressive array of organically developed processes and sub-processes that characterize your collective expertise). While you may have elegant new technologies facilitating the flow of information, the choices for how that information flows will still have the echoes and flavor of your company's first sale or filing cabinet. Your organization's distinctive traits are far less often the result of a master plan than a series of organically developed micro-processes piled atop each other.

To continuously improve an organization's processes, it is essential to make small incremental changes that mitigate exceptions, address potentially negative inputs or complications (exceptions, errors, or new constraints such as regulation), and accumulate and amplify positive outcomes.

An emergent change is a small workaround or adaptation in the performance or flow of work because of a specific and timely need or opportunity.

A need could occur because a team member encounters an impasse in an existing process. It could be that the process doesn't account for some new or different scenario, input, or exception or that they cannot intuitively determine how to resolve such an obstacle even if an acceptable workaround already exists. In other words, it could be a process shortcoming, or it could be a training issue. An opportunistic example of the emergence of a workaround could be when a team member sees a way to improve an end product or service quickly and believes they have the power to do so.

In either case, the worker will devise a workaround that helps them get the job accomplished or accomplished in a better way. If the workaround achieves that desired goal, then the worker may make the change part of their new personal work routine. Routine workarounds or adaptations may be visible or invisible, and the visible workarounds will likely influence future planned change.

As defined in Chapter One, the Japanese phrase "going to the Gemba" is often used in process improvement. In police work, it implies "going to where the crime occurred." It is also frequently used to suggest that the most valuable information regarding how a process currently operates or could be improved can be ascertained by going to where the deed is done. We can take that one step further and say that more significant potential is available to an organization that empowers the person doing the work to improve their parts of a larger process. We are not suggesting that everyone who works on a factory line is capable of "systems thinking." Still, we have experienced that many people in the trenches of an average organization do have that capability but are never empowered to apply it. The workers who don't have that ability are still valuable sources of feedback about how work is done. The organizations that determine how to unlock this potential will lead the future.

The term "strategic framework" in the context of process improvement means an overarching guidance. That combines clear vision, clear rules, clear objectives, and usable technical controls. We do not want to empower someone who only works in new client onboarding to create a new product or change our cybersecurity systems. However, we want to empower them to make incremental improvements within their operational domains. They are often most capable of streamlining the workflow between their inputs (customer info and order details) and outputs (a new, fully onboarded, and vetted client with an official account number).

The Concept of a Framework

Within a framework, a clear vision lets the organization know what they are trying to accomplish and what they want their coral reef to roughly look like in one, three, and five years.

Clear rules enable bright contributors to know what the required inputs and outputs are (we receive Accredited Investor Attestations, and we certify them by doing steps X and Y) and provide them with the ability to streamline the work between those various points, so long as they do not violate the rules.

Clear objectives should resemble statements such as, "We want to accelerate customer approvals without increasing customer risk."

And finally, usable technical controls ensure that people empowered to help produce positive change are tightly constrained to only make changes within their domain without creating unnecessary barriers to the changes they are allowed to make. Non-repudiable auditing of who makes changes becomes necessary to balance this empowerment with clear individual accountability.

Emergence is a scientific term for the way systems and ecosystems naturally emerge. Humans will naturally replicate this form of process improvement if they are empowered to do so. Brave leaders who desire to leverage continuous process improvement to accelerate their organizations will find great potential within this concept.

Traditional versus Emergent process improvements

Let's examine the typical relationship between friction, productivity, and time in the traditional model and then consider how it functions within the emergent model. The differences are subtle and highly dependent upon the agility inherent in how an organization improves its work. Still, the long-term benefits are substantial, and with the proper care and feeding, they can offer a perpetual return on investment.

Figure 1: Typical Process Improvement:

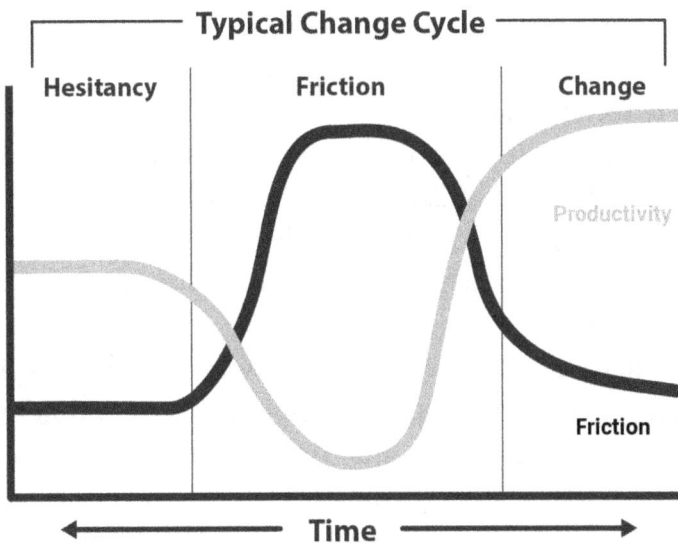

Typical Change Cycle

Hesitancy   **Friction**   **Change**

Productivity

Friction

Time

As you examine Figure 1, you will see that the Y-axis has two variables graphed: Friction and Productivity.

On the X-axis, we have Time broken into three distinct periods. Anyone who has ever managed process change will quickly recognize these and likely wince as we dig into the first two.

The first stage is "Wait and See." Remember, we are discussing typical (Big Bang) process improvement efforts. Your organization has a low trust level for the outcomes they are about to experience. Don't take that personally. People at *most* organizations have low trust in Big Bang process improvements. Why? Experience. And that experience dictates that when they hear claims of an exciting new change, they should "wait and see." Accordingly, this is when trust is relatively low, but so is friction. The change has not yet been implemented. Users may be nervous about the coming change, but it is not impacting them yet. Productivity is average. That is not where management wants to be. How do we know? They wouldn't have approved the process improvement effort if they were happy with the status quo.

The second stage is "Friction." The exact triggers for this stage will differ from organization to organization and project to project. Still, a familiar story is that beta testers for the new system tell people at the water cooler, "We have to do double data entry, and the new system is really confusing." That is where that low trust turns into active fear and concern. People who believe they can barely keep up with their jobs begin to proactively complain to their supervisors that they don't want to use the new system because they hear it is slowing people down. Nervous managers who are not clear about the benefits of the new system worry about the decline in productivity or morale of their teams. That can be a frustrating time for someone trying to orchestrate a beneficial process improvement. They are bringing something that should be viewed as beneficial but instead is being actively resisted.

There is a second component to the friction stage. We often see middle and senior management quite surprised when the rollout of a new system reduces productivity, sometimes significantly, during this phase. Things missed in a Big Bang implementation's discovery phase are now being discovered at the cost of lower productivity for early adopters.

Part 3 of this book, The Process of Process Improvement, will provide specific guidance on identifying ideal early adopters. If you have not selected your early adopters correctly, your response may range from diminished output to outright rebellion. Management may be inclined to communicate harshly with their process improvement team at this stage. That should be avoided because few things can hamper a problematic change effort as quickly as causing the core implementers of that change to feel demoralized and quit while that change is still struggling to take flight.

This friction phase is fraught with danger. Users are concerned. Managers are worried. Sponsoring executives feel pressure. Customers can sense that something is wrong, too. The good news is that productivity will recover if the organization has the will to continue through the change process and keeps the right people on board and engaged. Friction will also decline as the new system achieves adoption and its issues are resolved. That requires significant commitment at all levels.

This book will share numerous discovery and change communication best practices to help mitigate these risks and friction levels. That said, it is essential to remember that this graph, built on decades of experience, represents the unavoidable reality of change projects. Productivity will decrease while systems change. Friction will increase when people are asked to absorb that change. Going into a change with your eyes wide open to these facts will allow your organization to coalesce and sustain the willpower necessary to make it through to the intended positive outcomes.

The third phase is the "Change State." You will only reach this positive state if you endure and overcome the friction state. Once you have developed workarounds in your newly deployed system that have addressed the majority of unforeseen exceptions or missed requirements, friction will decline naturally. When the new system is successful enough that the old system can be retired, then double entry will no longer oppose your efforts at achieving organic user adoption.

Unfortunately, post-friction user adoption is sometimes achieved by paving over an unsuccessful change with new people. In other words, as discussed previously, there are scenarios where success is claimed at the cost of much human capital and tribal knowledge.

Having reached this final state one way or the other, most leadership teams will take a deep breath and a considerable pause before contemplating their next big change. But in the marketplace, there are always competitors. They refuse to sleep. Even if you have passed one of them, another awakes in the middle of the night with an idea of how to pass you. That is the real challenge to the slow pace of traditional change.

Fear not! There is a better way. Sometimes, you may need to leverage large-scale traditional change management or process improvement methodologies (i.e., big bang) to get your growing organization to an acceptable new starting point. But we will show you how to quickly migrate that one-time necessary big-bang effort into an agile, repetitive, iterative, and ongoing virtuous process-improvement cycle. In this better model, you will make a higher number of smaller and incrementally beneficial changes that more closely resemble the natural process of emergence.

Let's look at a different version of the same graph based on what we have seen when organizations implement emergent change management philosophies across time.

Figure 2: Emergent Process Improvement:

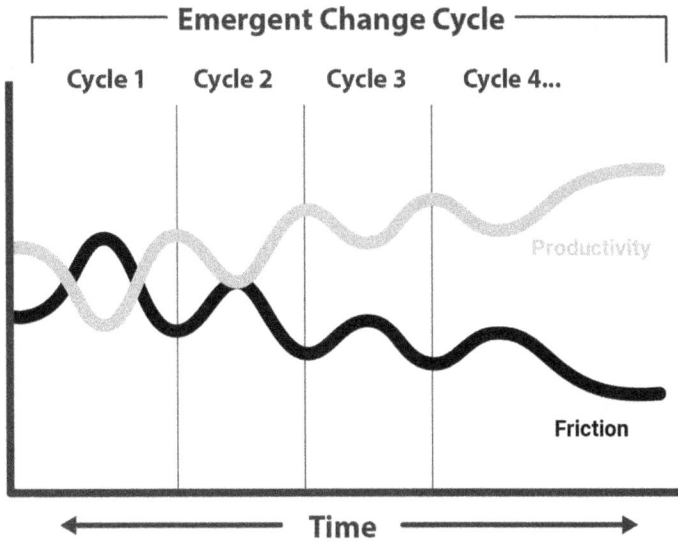

In Figure 2, you can see that we are tracking the same attributes on our X and Y axes. To claim that this model removes friction would be a lie. You may not be implementing a wholesale "Big Bang" change, but you are implementing a significant change to set up a new agile process improvement methodology. Because that process should theoretically be much faster, the friction and productivity cycle for that first change should also be more rapid. As a caveat to that, we have seen that some organizations can make *anything* take a long time, but even they can benefit from these techniques.

Once the organization's management and workers trust that a new system can quickly implement, sustain, and foster ongoing beneficial change, there will be a shorter and faster cycle between friction and productivity with each subsequent change. Once the organization gains trust for these enhanced and accelerated capabilities, the friction for each subsequent change will also incrementally decrease. Gains in productivity will also oscillate across shorter wavelengths. Because the changes are smaller and shorter in duration, so are the temporary adverse effects on productivity. That is part of the reason friction is reduced. Less time is required to reach the virtuous state, so there is less corollary fear about engaging in each additional change.

One of our large financial services clients, a global wealth and fund management leader, has built a center of excellence that frequently changes its internal processes in open and real-time collaboration sessions with its end users and stakeholders. They have gone from seeing an initial need for process standardization and control in one area of the business to a mature state of having hundreds of well-defined and well-controlled processes now operating in parallel within a common agile system that allows contributors to see various types of requests within a common framework and interface.

As all their work moving through these workflows is now traced, they can easily leverage the benefits of other processes already configured. For instance, if someone needs to track expenses while setting up a new fund, the person responsible for that specific fund can approve the expenses. The existing process of tracking personal expenses can be re-leveraged with slight modifications to become an additional component of the "new fund setup" process. When the person approving these expenses realizes there is too much work for them to do alone, the process can be quickly amended. The workflow can be updated to spread the approval requests across a responsible team, and the process can continue to run unchanged for both the person making the requests and the person in accounting who reimburses those expenses. That is an example of an emergent process change. A simple need is discovered "at the Gemba," a small beneficial change is made that keeps their proverbial coral reef growing and improving. This kind of agility does require significant upfront change. An organization will need to implement an agile system. They will also need to ensure that it creates the ability for responsible contributors and stakeholders to directly make (or achieve with minimal support) small, incremental, and beneficial changes without impacting the organization or other teams.

Now, for a rare shameless plug: If you use HighGear to build your foundation for agile process improvement, you would be able to empower business analysts and technically creative end users (who used to document their requirements and hand them to a programmer to complete) to securely achieve these kinds of agile changes on their own in record time.

The art of discovery

One of our early discovery engagements was with a group of end users, team leads, directors, and executives from a midsize publicly traded company. We started with an exercise to "quickly" record what our client did so that we could configure workflow automation to support their work. That turned out to be a challenging project, but it is also a salient example of how complex it can be to synchronize a sizeable multi-disciplined team's work and how significantly each group's or person's perceptions of that overall work process can vary.

Within minutes of starting the meeting, it became clear that each person had a largely job-specific perspective. More precisely, they lacked specific data on the bigger picture of how their team did what it did. To make better use of the time, we decided to interview four groups separately:

- the end users
- the team leads
- the department heads or directors
- the executives

Our goal in each case was to determine the information they believed was critical to capture or display as we automated the flow of work around their organization. Each session, taken on its own, seemed helpful. There would be a bit of disagreement among end users regarding what was important to capture or display at various steps, but we could relatively quickly get the group to come to a consensus.

What they did

This firm was managing information about surgical equipment to help normalize and standardize the terminology between customers and vendors. This organization had found a market for itself in making it easier for a hospital to order a specific type of surgical equipment and to be able to compare apples to apples even though various manufacturers and distributors failed or refused to follow industry-standard formats for the naming or SKU identification of these numerous products (i.e., the UNSPC codes).

Some manufacturers were on board. They realized that standardizing access to their products would increase demand. They wanted to make sure hospital buyers could find their products, and in many cases, they were willing to rename, relabel, or re-SKU their products if that would help. Many of these independent manufacturers had custom-built their products over the years and didn't realize they might have already matched an existing industry-standard SKU. Accordingly, they found value in the services of the firm we were working with. That firm could help them better align their products with existing market demand. Imagine renaming your product and selling more of it immediately. What vendor wouldn't be on board with that?

In this case, hospitals and their buyers were very much on board, too. They often needed specialty equipment and believed only one vendor could provide it. By interacting with this firm's "exchange," they discovered numerous similar or exact match alternatives, giving them a far more predictable and competitive supply chain. It was a data-driven exercise in the commoditization of a previously disaggregated market.

End users need data

Our end-user community included several roles: Analysts and Data Specialists in the U.S. and assistant analysts employed by an overseas partner firm.

The end users reported that completing any standardization efforts escalated for human intervention would require at least one photograph of the product. While, at times, the detailed product descriptions might give an analyst enough information to correlate various products, that was neither consistent nor reliable. For instance, if one manufacturer had produced a product called a "Titanium, knurled handle, 1 ½ inch surgical knife," and another manufacturer had a product listed as "Knurled handle, titanium, surgical knife, 1 ½ inch blade," these products may appear to be a match. However, a quick look at them may reveal they are quite different. One may offer a curved handle with a 90° angled blade, while the other may have a straight handle and a straight blade with a 90° angle only at the tip. These would be two items and reference two distinct UNSPCs.

The end users, familiar with these nuanced differences and the need to discern between them, innately understood the level of detail required to avoid a slowdown in their process. Once we inventoried all those data requirements, we inquired about their process.

An engagement might typically include a "data dump" of several hundred or several thousand items a manufacturer could produce. A cross-functional team of end users was assigned to standardize this information for each engagement. Their work was shared across several continents and time zones. They had lower-cost offshore facilities that processed the obvious exact matches. Analysts in the United States were processing the more nuanced potential matches, and they had data specialists (theoretically) looking for problems in the records to see which were automatically reconcilable before putting the remaining records into the manual entry or human reconciliation steps.

Examples of incoming data problems included discovering multiple unique products provided with the same or no image. There were also scenarios where product descriptions did not match the images, showing likely data import problems. There were also data cleanliness issues where a manufacturer had provided data precisely as requested or found in their system but failed to export a critical informational flag that might have shown this product was discontinued for as many as 20 years.

These painful experiences motivated the end users to demand potentially unattainable clarity in their incoming data. After all, if possible, that would streamline their jobs and make things easier for them. That is an understandable request. The nuance comes in determining what is a *must-have*, what is a *should-have*, what is a *could-have*, and what is a *won't-have*.

This model of categorization of requirements is known as the MoSCoW model. That is a simple acronym to help teams remember how to organize data or functional requirements into appropriate levels of importance.

Discovery with this first group (of end users) was certainly detailed. It was also reasonably straightforward. Focused on the data that would help streamline their jobs, they wanted as much of it as possible to be provided to them in advance, with a higher degree of accuracy than they had experienced. Their stories included time losses when large teams would meet to address adverse outcomes, often requiring the involvement of mid- and senior-level management. The potential mitigation of these reactive time losses presented some of the highest cost savings available by getting this process right.

The team leads need visibility.

The concerns changed when we got to our second group, the team leads. The team leads were more interested in ensuring the system would render metrics to help them see which data normalization processes were flowing well and which were at risk. They also wanted visibility into the workload of individual contributors to help them balance the flow. That was typical but excellent input, allowing us to consider the key metrics they cared about. We planned to timestamp and record various milestones and use them to build intuitive visualizations to reveal when those things were off-track. For instance, if an analyst had reviewed 300 records daily, this was considered a productive day.

Productivity is a relative metric. For instance, analysts could have 'very productive days' while the process still fell behind or created a backlog if the incoming rate was 600 records per day. This reality dictated that we needed to record both when these analysts had completed their normalization of exception records and how many records had entered their queue in each of the same work periods. These were straightforward exercises in discovery and analysis. We needed to consider and capture the data that would need to be recorded behind the scenes. That would facilitate our team leaders' need for visibility. We would also consider how to report on that information to operationalize it as work progressed.

So far, so good!

The department heads needed meaningful analytics

Next, we brought in the department heads. We wanted to ensure that these directors had an opportunity to share their priorities with us. They needed to see bottlenecks, obstacles, or performance problems, so we needed to ensure the capture of additional data to reflect the metrics they valued.

Department heads' requirements are often as simple as aggregating the same metrics their subordinate team leads require. However, it is also common for those responsible for more extensive parts of an operation to want access to analytics that provide deeper insights into the performance of their teams in ways that are irrelevant to the individual teams. For the most part, this specific example was a straightforward exercise of ensuring we had captured the objective metrics needed to correctly reflect the patterns underlying the events, milestones, or conditions they reported needing to see as key performance indicators (KPI) or metrics.

We also worked up conceptual dashboards and proactive reporting for the benefit of those operational leaders. It was unlikely that they would have time or occasion to log into the system, so they needed summary-level information with easy-to-understand visualizations emailed to them frequently enough to keep them informed but not so often as to become noise. This part of the session also went pretty much as expected.

Bring in senior management.

While many perceive senior management (C-Suite, organizational heads, etc.) as disconnected and detached, it was surprising how well-informed they were regarding what their team leads and various levels of managers wanted regarding metrics and accountability. There was a surprisingly clear alignment regarding how the organization wanted to measure itself. That cascaded down from the top with an atypical level of clarity. However, that clarity hit a dead end right there.

A difference of perceptions.

As a diligent quality control, we asked each group we did discovery with for their perspectives on how each area under their control completed their work. The gaps that emerged were surprising. We diligently recorded each subsequent group's conceptual views of the overall workflow on a paper flipchart, as we had initially done with the end users.

Though impressively in sync on metrics and goals, our senior management team was equally out of sync with their organization's workflow. They confidently and quickly shared while we furiously diagrammed their perceived workflows onto another flipchart. They believed most of their work was done through automation via the more technical end users in their US office (i.e., the data experts). Those data experts were busy cleaning up imports and often felt overwhelmed trying to keep up with demand. They were not processing much, if any, of the data automatically, nor had they gotten around to working on the automation.

Senior management also believed that their overseas or offshore partner's resources handled the exceptions so that their "internal people" would not be slowed down. They thought their internal people, specifically the analyst teams (i.e., the medical product subject matter experts), were also primarily working with customers to help define and streamline import and export requirements as they built the exchange.

In summary, this organization's highest leadership had close to no idea what was going on from the time they engaged their client until the time clients' information ended up in their exchange.

The first benefit of discovery - getting reconciled

The exchange this organization had created facilitated a market-changing paradigm shift. Still, loading the medical world's messy data into their system was far more daunting than most of the organization had perceived. That was because each stakeholder group only saw a specific portion of the bigger picture. We could help them reconcile these varying perceptions around how their work was accomplished. However, we first needed to help them understand why the different perceptions were so problematic.

Absent from our interviewees, we taped the various flipchart workflow diagrams onto the wall around the outer edge of a conference room. As we looked at these diagrams, one obvious pattern emerged. But it was not a workflow pattern. It was also not a lack of expertise in what they did. Instead, they had no idea how work was getting done across their organization. Some of the data we had gotten from team leads seemed arguably accurate, but it conflicted with what their end users thought was happening. Similar conflicts were apparent between the team leads, directors, and senior management.

You may have heard the saying, "A frog in a well only sees a small portion of the sky." If you ask a frog in a well about the weather, he might tell you it is a clear, beautiful day marked by blue skies and ample sunshine. If you were to lift that frog out of the well, he might look surprised when he realized a furious summer storm was on the horizon's edge. However, that information was not available to the frog when his perspective was biased because he was at the bottom of the well.

That perspective problem is why we will modify the generally correct directive of "go to the Gemba" to say, more accurately, "always *start* at the Gemba." Much of the best information came from the end users closest to the work being done. However, some things happened with handling exceptions that our "frogs in the well" could not see correctly. If we had taken their advice alone, we would've been significantly off course, especially if we had built rigid or brittle solutions based on that input alone.

At the end of this process, which had now taken more than two full days, we needed to make representatives from each stakeholder group aware of the challenge we had discovered. We brought them all into the room, where we covered the varied flowcharts with blank pieces of paper of equal size. We asked the group, "How many of you believe you are all roughly on the same page regarding how work flows across your process of onboarding and normalizing data?" They *all* put their hands up. Without making any derogatory remarks, we quietly took the paper that we had taped over the workflow diagrams away one at a time. As we went around the room, we could see the looks on people's faces changing. They realized the challenge we had, and it was painful to watch. They had no idea what they were doing!

Our client embraced the challenge and pressed forward, now wiser. The first value of discovery is reconciling with the truth and the transformational opportunity it brings to get everyone on the same page. We may have been off to a rough start. Still, when you consider the implications of building automation to facilitate incorrect assumptions, a rough start (in discovery) is far better than a rough ending when your new system or change is getting rolled out.

Key takeaways.

We're going to dig further into the art of discovery, but let's wrap this first pass up with a few key takeaways:

- End users typically offer the most nuanced detail about what can go wrong with individual work transactions as they flow across a company's process.
- Those who manage the flow of work can typically offer meaningful insights and perspectives into how errors, exceptions, and unexpected nuances get handled.

- It is not uncommon for the perspectives of these first two groups to differ. It does not mean that one is correct and the other is wrong. They simply bring you different perspectives on the same data, but they must be reconciled early in your process.
- It is critical to work with management and determine the key metrics and milestones that must be recorded or observed. Building recordation of those metrics and milestones into a process early on will ensure that management's big-picture expertise can be leveraged to help you iteratively improve the process after it goes live.
- Leave more time than you think you need for discovery, and don't assume that everyone will be on the same page.
- It is vital to gather all the information possible before designing systems, and it is essential to build agile systems that can quickly change. The ultimate test of your discovery will be the deployment of your solution. If your launch state is brittle or hard to change, it may fail when just one or two details are wrong.

Less talk, more metrics!

We can't fix something until we can see it. We have already given an example of how you can take four teams into discovery and get four different versions of what they do. So, how do we solve that? Where possible, we go from verbal and visual discovery (e.g., written documents and workflow diagrams) to empirical discovery.

The answer to this age-old problem is *agile systems*. If an organization can build something quickly with loosely defined constraints, it can measure and monitor the flow of work within that lightweight framework. That empowers an organization's discovery efforts with empirical data. There is no more effective means of getting your various teams to agree on how things are done than 60- or 90-days' worth of empirical data recording precisely how things were done.

"We did not know exactly how many requests were coming into [our part of the city's operation] at any given time nor what the statuses were. With metrics, I now know exactly what's happening, what our workload is, and there are times that we need to make changes to meet the demand."
—Omer S., Operations Chief,
one of the largest cities in the U.S.

We've gone into organizations and done discovery where people have told us things like, "We get 30 or 40 exceptions a day, and "Jack" has to handle them all." However, after we built a lightweight system to track the work going through that process, teams were often surprised to discover that while 'Jack' was handling 30 or 40 items a day, very few were exceptions. Most were actually cases where anyone could have done the work, but there were three or four each day that only Jack could do because of his specialized training and experience.

Even Jack thought he had done much more of the specialized exception work. Why? He had long seen reports showing that he completed roughly 30 or 40 cases daily. But most of what he could remember was the grueling effort to resolve cases where the information provided was incomplete or inaccurate. It consumed most of his time. We could still help them solve the problem, but it was not the same problem the organization previously believed it had.

Another organization we worked with had roughly 1200 daily requests flowing through their business process. They were confident all these items had to go to a dispatcher who would review them and assign them to people. That was the intended process. Management believed it, and the dispatcher also thought that was how it was going. The dispatcher and her managers hadn't realized that when their team reached about 500 requests daily, many specialists had begun self-selecting work out of the queue. The dispatcher was still looking at items in the queue and routing them to various specialists, so the dispatcher (functioning as our proverbial 'frog in the well') only saw their perspective. She was logging in frequently and moving things from a general queue to the work queues of individual specialists. Similar to Jack, in our prior example, our dispatcher saw reports showing 1200 requests going through the system daily. Therefore, it's easy to understand how she would put those two bits of information together and retain the belief that she was overwhelmed routing 1200 tasks per day to the various specialists to do the work when, in fact, she was struggling to keep up with just the 500 or so she was still manually routing. But remember that all of this is still based on the discovery interviews we performed with various stakeholders – each a frog in their own well.

The team members knew that the dispatcher was still routing work to them. However, they also knew that she would consider how much work they already had assigned to them via a high-level report analyzing the percentage of work associated with each specialist. Diligent specialists were self-assigning tough cases they knew they were qualified for. However, some of their newer or less-informed specialists were just grabbing whatever looked easy. That meant others were getting most of the tough cases or work the dispatcher manually routed. She probably would have noticed the pattern if she had the time, but she had begun to develop a concern that some of her team never seemed to be fully clearing their queue of the work assigned to them.

That may sound like chaos, but most unautomated flows of work endure similar chaos because of perceptions that conflict with reality. We could have built a sophisticated system to capture every bit of data necessary for everyone to make well-informed decisions. We could have built every dashboard metric the various stakeholders were confident they required. That would have been easy to do. But we would have been building all that atop a significant stack of deeply flawed information.

In contrast, if we were standing all of this up in an agile system, we would have the advantage of implementing a lightweight system for tracking and assignment and then using it to gather facts. And who wouldn't want to start with facts?

By implementing a lightweight system and getting the users on board with the prospective benefit of starting with facts, we can stand something up in a matter of days that allows an organization to track all the work coming through their process – at a high level. We create clear user benefits by quickly providing the information they need to respond to each request at their fingertips. Stage one is simply to deploy a repository of the required information (no better or worse than the stack of information they had before today, but now easier to find). That will also benefit the organization and process owners by quickly providing a ground-level mechanism to record and track the inception and advancement of work as it flows through their processes.

Back to our example, after 30 days of doing just what we have described here, many of the organization's leaders were astounded by their new emerging realities. It made sense to wait another 30 days to ensure this trend continued and that we would not make decisions based on a potential anomalous period.

Their most surprising discovery was that the organization was not handling anywhere near 1200 cases daily. Their peak day across the entire 60-day period was closer to 700. They had roughly doubled their estimation of how much work was being done and underestimated how much person-time each transaction consumed by half.

No invoices were generated for this internal work, so the transaction count had to come from other sources. There were records of how many emails had come in, and somewhere along the way, an understandable assumption had developed that each email represented a case. However, many cases had numerous follow-up emails requesting or providing additional information requested by a specialist or were often from the requestor checking in for a status update.

Another example of unexpected data was the average time it took to complete a satisfactory response for each request. More subject matter expertise was also being applied to some of these cases than had previously been understood. There were also far more cases that were being self-assigned to individuals who were underqualified to complete the case accurately, thereby requiring work to be passed around the organization before being correctly completed. That might include hallway wanderers looking for a more senior person with an open door – thus invisibly consuming the time of two contributors with one case.

Other examples revealed highly qualified individuals working on cases that more junior people could have easily and quickly completed.

In this example, there were plenty of problems worth solving and benefits to be gained, but they were different problems than what the organization believed they had when we arrived. They had correctly identified symptoms, but an accurate diagnosis of root causes required empirical diagnostics not previously available.

Most of us would never want a doctor to prescribe a course of harsh, risky, or painful treatments for a medical condition without first empirically validating that we had the associated malady. However, it is surprising how often the corporate equivalent is undertaken by well-intended people who are convinced they understand their organization's problems by virtue of a limited view as our proverbial frog in a well.

We have also seen people push a solution to bolster their resumes, regardless of whether they can validate the need, and we have observed cases where people discovered their teams were far more productive than they were giving them credit for. Empirical data shows us where teams need training to deal with certain types of problems or where large-scale processes may not be broken but simply need more effective exception management to help clear the backlog.

Capture and Display

Organizations and the individuals that make them up have a pretty good sense of the data they need to make decisions. We think of these elements as "capture and display." We ask our various stakeholders, "What data do we need to capture at each stage?" We also ask, "What data will we need to display at each stage to ensure that people can make the right decisions to complete their work or move it to the next stage?" At each new stage, we need to ask these same questions again.

Here are a few more specific examples:

- Suppose a contributor in our team completes a quality assurance step on every 10th record. Do we need them to attach something, enter data to provide context for their findings, or prove they completed the quality assurance control?
- Will an auditor require information that validates that a client-initiated a request even if it has been entered into our system by an internal employee?

These are the kinds of things that we need to think about capturing and displaying:

- Who will we capture this data from?
- To whom do we need to display it, and when will they need it?

Sessions (and questions) aimed at gathering these 'capture and display' elements are where verbal and visual discovery sessions often become incredibly effective and insightful. High-level workflow diagrams are beneficial artifacts that aid in the capture of discovery sessions.

But nothing, including the very best of fact-gathering questions, beats empirical data. If you can build a lightweight system quickly and run it for a period, you will give yourself an edge over everyone who gathers data through subjective means because yours will have been gathered objectively. We've seen it time and time again. Objective data is king, while the very best of subjective data remains just that: subjective.

The frog in the pot

Consider the age-old metaphor about frogs thrown into a pot of boiling water. They will likely leverage their jumping abilities to escape the pot. The validity of this claim has now been disproven via vital scientific work, surely funded by taxpayers who couldn't sleep without the answer. Nonetheless, the adage stipulated that when placed into a pot of water at room temperature that was then slowly heated, the frogs wouldn't recognize the subtle change and would end up getting cooked.

Thus, the point of the metaphor (whether settled science or not) is to boil the frog slowly because the point behind the metaphor remains solid in the areas of business process.

We have observed that small financial services organizations with as few as 15 or 20 employees who take the time to build smooth processes can easily outperform competitors that are five, ten, or even twenty times their size. Contrary to what might be assumed, operational excellence is not the domain of large companies; it is the domain of leading companies. Your personal experience as a customer will be defined by the processes supporting the companies you do business with.

Look for the areas that slow you or your team down and find ways to measure them accurately and improve them incrementally. We will sound like a broken record with this advice, but there is a reason for the repetition. Small and incremental changes based on facts are quickly recognized as beneficial changes. Thus, your team can easily absorb and even learn to welcome those changes. Rather than throwing the proverbial frog into boiling water, you will turn up the heat slowly as you refine how your organization does business. New people will join and learn those systems. You will not break the workarounds your existing people have developed in areas you have not explored because you have not created a "big bang." You have looked for places where incremental improvements can naturally emerge as your business improves with them.

Small business tip: As an entrepreneur or 'Swiss Army Knife leader,' you know your business well, but you're probably too expensive and busy to do all the work yourself. Even if you decide to take on your first process improvement effort yourself, be sure to take a bright team member with you through the entire process. Process improvement will make your business stand out, and you will soon need to be able to delegate and have them repeat this for you as often as possible and wherever you see the need or opportunity.

Remember if there are two great teams, the one with the better processes will win. Therefore, if your organization does not currently possess the skills needed for continuous and agile process improvement, you should start resolving that now if you want to grow.

Section Summary:
Dispelling the Myth of the Empire Builder.

Many leaders believe they can single-handedly ascertain everything their organization (or part of the organization) needs and successfully introduce a new and better plan or system all at once. Some will succeed, but most will not. Some will claim to have succeeded over time, but an honest assessment would show that these organizations experienced high levels of stress enduring those "successes." As organizations work to fix the flaws in their "big bang" implementations, they often fail to realize that the actual cost of chaotic change is not just lost time, consultant fees, or reputations but organizational morale and the impact on their employees and customers.

The alternative is to create baseline operational systems that include agility and the ability to gather and analyze facts quickly. Making small incremental changes based on facts will deliver superior user adoption and outcomes while engaging the organization to learn and think as a team.

PART THREE

THE PROCESS OF PROCESS IMPROVEMENT

The specific methods we are about to ask you to undertake, for many, will be an entirely new way of thinking about process improvement. Therefore, it is reasonable to ask. Will this work for me?

We are about to move on to the ten steps we assert are all vital for achieving unprecedented ROI and adoption in your process improvement efforts. Lest you wonder if these numerous steps are worth the effort, we want to share some encouragement from others ahead of you on the same road.

"With the support of the HighGear team, they give us best practices, the best way to approach a certain problem, to find the right solution…And if you follow and implement their best practices, you'll find that it's easy actually to come back in and make minor adjustments or add a new feature that your workflow may have missed before. It's seamless."

—Bruce L., Business Analyst, Defense Manufacturer

"The impact to our team using [the HighGear methodology] has been like going from a horse and buggy to a Ferrari. Everybody uses it. It also provides an added benefit of business continuity. We program stability through the workflow, which drives the best behaviors."

—Don T., Engineering Lead,
Top 5 global technology company

"[This system] has helped the team grow professionally. We have several younger managers, and it's helped them focus on the process. As you mature as a business, it helps you think about how to organize teams and workloads that must go through the process."

—Kathy S., Senior Manager (Business Operations/
Financial Services), Global Motorsports Brand

"I think [that capability] has allowed me to succeed in the organization. It's given me the ability to provide my internal customers with the capabilities they need. So that reflects on me and my team. It's been an enabler for us. It's allowed us to standardize workflows, easily change workflows, and adapt quickly as business needs change. And that is looked at very positively."

—Jeff C., Information Technology Leader,
Multinational Insurance Carrier

"…To quantify my sanity is not measurable, but that is definitely impacted by the process improvements we have completed. I don't have to worry about the boss saying, "Hey, why did we drop this ball? I just do not have the anxiety of wondering what's out there; instead, I have the feeling of having control over the situation and knowing what people have on their desks. That is not measurable or quantifiable, but it's extremely important to me."

—Lisa C., Director of Operations, Private Equity, Real Estate Investment Firm

CHAPTER FIVE

DESIGNING A BETTER FUTURE

The person who believes something is impossible should never interrupt the person doing it.
—Unknown

Process improvement can be broken into three categories:

1) The first category is **organic process improvement**. Organic process improvements are the natural workarounds people put in place to make their jobs easier. They are not necessarily coherent on a larger scale or beneficial to the broader organization. However, much organizational value is stored in the information and outcomes associated with these organic workarounds.

These emergent or organic processes are typically not automated and are often sufficient until a certain point. Challenges arise when an organization needs to hire new people quickly. Growth-oriented hiring is frequently done because the volume of work is increasing rapidly. That makes it more urgent to smooth out complex operations so the organization can continue to deliver consistent customer experiences as it grows. Organic processes can be challenging to analyze, making identifying opportunities for improving efficiency more difficult. For this reason, agile thinking and a process-focused mindset will quickly become an asset to organizations that understand the importance of process improvement and a liability to organizations that don't.

2) The second category is **the organized improvement and automation of specific processes**. Coalescing our previously organic processes into coherent, large-scale, and well-defined processes is typically done to facilitate the collection of large amounts of information or artifacts. That kind of effort is generally undertaken to help streamline more significant swathes of work or workflows so that systems and people can intelligently act upon that information at scale. The scope of an initial undertaking of this kind is akin to designing a city intentionally rather than growing it organically over decades.

Picture an old village where someone built a home that later became a restaurant or tavern, encouraging others to build their homes and businesses nearby. What emerges is a mix of different widths of streets, various sizes of buildings, and a map that looks like a series of pretzels have fallen on the floor.

Contrast that to the city of Indianapolis, Indiana. Designers laid the whole city out in a grid ahead of time. By simply checking whether a street name starts with East or West, you will know whether that address is on the east or west side of Meridian Street, which runs north and south through the city's center. Indianapolis is a designed city where the display of information conveys additional meaning because of that organization. If someone told you their address was 500 E. Bobcat St., you would immediately know they were five blocks west of Meridian Avenue, close to downtown, because the letters go up as you progress away from the city's center northward.

Imagine trying to establish that kind of structured grid over an older, organically developed city like Tarragona City in Spain. You'd have to disrupt a lot of homes and businesses to create an organized grid like that! Initial "professional" process improvement efforts can be like trying to accomplish that level of change. However, unleashing similar havoc in process improvement will sabotage user adoption and trust. That is why this next section will focus primarily on the efforts required to achieve that first change and why attempting to achieve it in meaningful increments is so critical.

3) The third category of process improvement is **Continuous Process Improvement**. We will significantly expand upon the best practices for making incremental changes later in the book. We will also cover building a center of excellence to keep those incremental improvements flowing. For now, suffice it to say that once your organization acclimates to making incremental changes and feels the benefits of those small, incremental, and ongoing beneficial changes or advancements, there will be less need for the kind of wholesale organizational change management and preparation required in the second category of process improvement.

Background I – Finding the Truth – A.K.A. Discovery

HighGear sells software that helps organizations quickly, iteratively, and radically improve their processes. Our software provides visibility into business processes, often producing valuable insights into how a business *should* work, and it makes it all look easy! But even we must resist when a prospect has the tempting idea, "This looks so easy that I should just map our entire business into this software now and *then* roll out the new solution next Monday."

Even if entertaining that possibility might lead to a more straightforward or significant sale for us, that quick sale might often be followed by our eager prospect orchestrating a Big Bang of their own, which rarely goes well. Accordingly, we have trained ourselves to push back on that idea.

The better path is to make small beneficial changes and gain trust that real or more extensive improvements are possible. If everyone agrees that a particular part of your organization has a broken process, and the people within that group are hungry for positive change, consider making small incremental improvements in that part of the organization first. We caution strongly against trying to orchestrate your smaller-scale big bang. Trying to determine everything a team does before deploying a new process or technology is often error-prone because you may still be dangerously light on facts. What we have seen as more productive, time and time again, is the humble path of just tracking the specifics you can see until additional provable facts emerge.

As covered earlier in the book, when we run discovery sessions with our clients, we often find that stakeholders disagree vigorously about how work flows across their organizations. Most find the differences surprising. That truth should be a red flag for anyone ready to implement change over a critical business process. It should also lead to the question, "How can we empirically determine the facts?"

> The Happy Path. Often used by Process Improvement Professionals, the term The Happy Path refers to the case where everything goes as expected (i.e., an ideal client ordering a standard product that you already have in stock and that is to be delivered to a standard address within a reasonable amount of time).

As previously discussed, we often find numerous organic workarounds when legacy systems don't work or work well. Suppose we examine the prior system and its "happy path" but fail to examine all those workarounds. In that case, we will be missing a significant portion of the information we need to effectively replace that system without creating breaks in the process. If we interview the stakeholders to find those workarounds and find inconsistencies in their perceptions, this is proof that we are still working with partial or inaccurate data.

If we start our discovery efforts from the top (i.e., with senior leadership), record the overarching organizational directives, and work our way down, we may discover people working around those cascading directives in the trenches. This resistance may be self-serving, but in our experience, it is more often well-intended. The teams in the trenches believe they are accomplishing leadership objectives by way of these necessary workarounds. The need for this is frequently justified by a belief that their leaders couldn't have foreseen the nuances involved in their work, and bricolage takes over. Most process improvement work starts from a dangerous starting point, e.g., missing, inconsistent, or flat-out wrong information or perspective. Thus, the key is to make the first step to gather empirical facts instead of subjective information.

The simplest way to gather empirical facts is to create an agile system that enables lightweight data collection. A team might say, "We get 50 tasks daily, and almost everything we get is wrong. All our work goes through this triage process, and Sammy must sign off on half of it." We can accept that premise and build a system or process to support it or first validate those assumptions. With the agility of modern technology, it is now possible for the unskilled but technically creative entrepreneur or team leader to build elementary systems that quickly facilitate creating a record for each bit of work that moves through a team. It doesn't matter whether you are a rancher tracking cattle, a landscaper tracking lawn work, or a Fortune 500 tracking the onboarding of sophisticated investors into a limited fund. What all these examples have in common is that you cannot begin to make progress until you know your starting point.

As-Is and To-Be

In process improvement, the As-Is state is where you find a process or problem when you arrive. It is the state you study and record, hoping to identify all the artifacts that must be captured, the workarounds that must be replicated, and the opportunities for improvement that may be identified through process discovery and analysis.

The To-Be state is the 'designed state' you hope to overlay via new policies, procedures, processes, or systems.

Given the widely accepted idea that the as-is state is the foundation of process improvement, you'd be surprised how many experts build their to-be design on a weak foundation of subjective data. We have seen the negative impacts of starting with subjective data within massive process improvement efforts at some of the largest companies around the world.

Empirical Fact Gathering

If you cut lawns, don't believe your team when they tell you how long it takes. Get a simple application to track the location of their phones and run a report on the difference between their arrival time at a particular customer's location and their departure. Now you have empirical data!

You can and will figure out how to apply this fact-gathering concept to your business. In fact, by the time you have finished this book, you will find yourself thinking in entirely new ways about discovery and how to make it empirical. When you have facts, you are already in a better starting position than most "process experts."

By creating simple fact-gathering systems and then creating small incremental improvements based on those facts, you will achieve the holy grail of process improvement: Continuous process improvement. But unlike most efforts where prior metrics are scarce, you will also have the data necessary to measure and prove the benefits and value of your incremental changes.

Consider a Fortune 500 onboarding sophisticated investors where that firm (subjectively) believes that 50% of their new clients come with significant complexity. That might justify a plan to hire more senior analysts. But what if, after empirical fact-gathering, we discover the perception that 50% of the applications were complex was created by a large backlog of work when, in fact, only 10% are complex? These new facts will help you make better improvements and apply them more effectively, leading to better business decisions.

When building a process that includes leadership's direction and the empirical facts from the front-line employees, we should include both parties while conducting our initial discovery. Leadership presence is not required in each discovery session after your initial kickoff session. They usually provide high-level direction but do not stay to "get into the weeds." We typically engage them again near our final discovery sessions to validate that our emerging to-be vision remains on course with their strategy. To start the discovery process, I recommend beginning with a 10,000-foot view. Although there may be many names for it, the idea of the 10,000-foot view is to start by reviewing the process needs at a high level. That allows all parties to agree on where the process will begin, where it will end, and the significant steps in between.

It may surprise you that we'll often walk into a first discovery session only to spend the remainder of that meeting discussing where the process should begin. In addition to identifying the steps of the process, the 10,000-foot view allows us to identify the actors, or roles, involved in the process. In the end, we have a document that identifies where we will begin, all the steps of the process, and the desired outcomes or endpoints. We can then use that high-level perspective to guide us through the remaining in-depth discovery work. An added benefit of starting with the 10,000-foot view is that it helps us manage our meetings by contrasting our progress on the details to the bigger picture we established at the start.

A quick note on documenting the process: It helps to use a tool that will allow you to build your process while conducting the discovery, especially if there is a visual workflow component to your solution. That is one of the powerful benefits of HighGear (and other solutions that provide visual workflow drafting tools); it is self-documenting and provides a visual representation of your process. That significantly helps your subject matter experts easily visualize the process you are helping them build.

The older, outdated, or legacy discovery model involves having a business analyst or someone with a similar skillset conduct discovery sessions, take copious notes, or use a word processor or visual workflow diagramming tool designed solely to describe a process. These legacy tools do not provide any solution development capabilities. For the analyst (or a developer) to start building a solution, they must start from scratch by transcribing that diagram or notation into some other form. In that model, it takes at least two times longer to produce the process because you are documenting it while conducting discovery but not making any progress toward building the process. With a modern visual workflow application such as HighGear, by the end of your discovery session, you should be to a point where your users may immediately or soon be able to test some parts of what you've already configured.

That feature set is a 4D Design Canvas™ because Discovery, Design, Deployment, and Documentation can all be completed within the same tool.

Now, when we dig into the more in-depth discovery, you'll want to break up the details on a per-step basis and document them. To start, you will do so at the beginning of the process and identify all the avenues through which new requests, cases, incidents, etc., will enter your process. For example, will users be logging into your system to create their requests, or will they be emailing or calling a contact on your team or utilizing some other automated method for making their request in your system? Next, you'll dig into the details for every step of the process:

1. What communication needs to happen at the beginning of this step? (should we notify the person now assigned to complete the work?)
2. What should the outcome of this step be?
3. Why do we complete this step the way we do it?
4. What should we call this step?
5. What information will a contributor require to perform this step?
6. What information must the user provide before completing this step?
   a. Are there any optional details users should be able to add?
7. What should we call the means of exiting this step?
8. Who is responsible for this step?
9. When should this step be completed? (or how long should it take?)
10. Who else may also need to see the record at this step?
11. Is there anything special that needs to happen at this step?
12. What communication needs to happen at the end of this step? (If another action must take place on another team, should we notify them? Are others awaiting notification that their case has reached this stage?)

Let's expand on each of these points just a bit.

1. What communication needs to happen at the beginning of this step?

   Our process may be the starting point for a simple task that will be opened and closed, or we may be the mid-point in a longer-running complex process that spans multiple teams or departments. In the former case, we may only need to notify the assigned contributor of a new requirement. In the latter case, we may also need to notify our current assignee. We may also need to inform a preceding group that our system has received the work and perhaps notify a subsequent contributor of the incoming requirement. We should also always consider when to notify the "customer of record" for each request. Over-notification becomes noise, but critical milestones may be desirable information for our stakeholders.

2. What should the outcome of this step be?

This question leads us to gather the details of what should happen at this step from the business perspective. We are asking ourselves the question, why are we doing this? What do we want or need to accomplish? In our warranty example, we'll want to consider the steps a quality assurance person will be doing, from receiving a request for an RMA (Return Manufacturer Authorization) to a conversation with the customer or dealer, etc., to receiving, processing, and inspecting the returned item and possibly replacing it, etc. Ultimately, we want to ensure that the procedures around each step support the dual objective of ensuring customer satisfaction while protecting sustainable profits. We need to address the customer's claim quickly. Still, suppose the inspection reveals a critical flaw in the design of an item, and we fail to address that. In that case, we may satisfy the customer with a quick response, but if the replacement part also fails, that satisfaction will be short-lived, and so will our profits.

3. Why do we complete this step the way we do it?

When examining a process's "as-is" state, this specific question is where you are most likely to discover or reveal workarounds. Here, you can evaluate how to eliminate or incorporate these bricolage-based fixes into a process's "to-be" state. An honest response to the why question may often be, "Because that's how we've always done it." That response (or statements with similar meanings) frequently indicates that you have uncovered an area where process improvement opportunities will likely exist. When the answers to "why?" are outcome or procedure-based, the specific steps you are inquiring about will typically be rooted in well-established policies, controls, or at least prior thought. But the "because this is the way we have always done it this way" type of answers often mask significant bricolage. That is an opportunity (and should be a warning sign) to slow down and extract all of the information you can ascertain about why things are being done in specific ways. Be sure to ask ample questions about exception cases and take copious notes. You will likely refer to this when contemplating your new and improved procedures.

4. What should we call this step?

That is usually an easy question for your contributors to answer, and the answer allows us to label this step when properly discussing a process's components. We may also need to define or name related metrics to facilitate reporting the steps within a process that a specific request or record has traversed and how long it may have spent in each step.

For example, in our warranty claims process, we may have the following step names (in the order they occur in the process):

Customer / Dealer requests RMA
Warranty Triage
RMA Adjudication
    RMA Approval
    RMA Rejection -> Invokes another process
    assigned to a senior QA resource
Item Return Label
Item Receipt (Shipping)
Inspection
Replacement/Refund
Redesign and testing (optional)

We may want to consider numbering our process steps to ensure they will are easy to sort or display in the desired order:

01 Customer / Dealer requests RMA
02 Warranty Triage
    03 RMA Adjudication
    03.1 RMA Approval
    03.9 RMA Rejection (Invokes another process assigned to a senior QA resource)
03.2 Item Return Label
03.3 Item Receipt (Shipping)
04 Inspection
05 Replacement/Refund
06 Redesign and testing (optional)

A leading zero, or multiple zeros, can help ensure that numerically identified steps exceeding "10" or "100," etc., still intuitively appear in your intended order when viewed through a third-party reporting package or application. Another option could be to create a Process Step Number field and place the corresponding numeric value into the field.

5. What information will a contributor require to perform this step?

When we ask this question, we seek to discover what information (both data and artifacts) we may need to attempt to collect or require further upstream. Identifying this list of data is usually organic and easy to do as your SME's (Subject Matter Exports) know what info they need to be able to do their work. However, it is also wise to carefully review and inventory any screens, forms, or other incoming media they may receive as part of completing a step in their "as-is" state. It is also critical to ask how they handle exceptions. Another thing to remember to ask is if there is other information they would like to see included to help streamline future exception handling.

6. What information must the user provide before completing this step?

When we ask what information our contributors need to gather and include before they complete this step, we aim to discover the data the user must provide to prove they have done their work correctly, according to policy or regulation, etc., or to support later contributors or steps. This data is often well-known to our SMEs, but the frequency of details being overlooked or taken for granted informs us that additional diligence is required. For instance, while our contributors are often aware of what the later parties in a multi-step process will require, we may need to expand our thinking to include capturing data for analytical or regulatory compliance purposes. In our warranty example's *03.9 RMA Rejection* step, we may need to add a facility for the inspector to include a photograph of the returned item supporting their adjudication that the item failed due to unintended use (such as a bent part neither designed nor warranted to perform in a weight-bearing capacity). This requirement adds accountability but will also support the senior quality personnel or salesperson who must interact with the client. In summary, we should consider and validate what data is required to save the record or complete the step and what data may be optional but beneficial if available.

7. What should we call the means of exiting this step?

When processes are being digitally transformed or enhanced, it is valuable to consider clear means of representing and communicating the change of state or status that moves a record or case from one state to another. Addressing that need is typically completed via generating meaningful state or stage gate names such as "approved," "not approved," or "more information required."

In our warranty example, we have a step with two intuitive exit states or statuses:

03 RMA Adjudication
03.1 RMA Approval
03.9 RMA Rejection (Invokes another process assigned to a senior QA resource)

Frequently, we would create two statuses to represent these options and record them for later analysis before moving each request to the next step, either the generation of an item return label (perhaps auto-completed) or the exiting of this request from our primary warranty process and possibly assigning the request to the account's salesperson or a senior quality assurance resource trained in how to communicate these kinds of exceptions back to the end client or dealer.

Recordation of these statuses (even if a request only remains there for a brief moment before being reassigned to another contributor or team) allows us to perform later analysis of how many claims go down each path. They also provide intuitive options for our contributors.

8. Who is responsible for this step?

When we ask who is responsible for this step, we're looking for what team, role, or individual should do the work at this step. In other words, we want to clarify the assignment and accountability.

9. When should this step be completed?

When we ask, "When should this step be completed?" we're looking for a means of assigning a Due Date or determining how long an item may linger within this step before requiring escalation. We're looking for when to notify stakeholders (e.g., the contributor or the requestor) that a request is falling behind, and we want to record to whom escalations should be sent if the delays persist. Wherever possible, there should be a Due Date for every process step or at least a recorded expectation for how long this step *should* take. In some processes, due dates are rigid values that cannot and should not be changed. In other processes, customers may treat due dates as "guidelines." We view that as a poor practice and will generally suggest renaming such guidance appropriately, such as desired ship date, etc. A due date should reflect when something will be completed. Diluting that meaning by using it in less rigid cases should be avoided.

Every step of a process should have its own Due Date. That can be auto-calculated as an item enters each step or pre-calculated by working backward from the overall due date.

Process contributors may push back that they don't have or need due dates for their steps. They may have used a system or method without due dates, SLA considerations, or capabilities, such as if a process were previously managed using emails. The concept may be foreign or concerning since email has no enforceable due date capacity. Our client's process professionals (as well as our own) often report statements like, "We have never had due dates, so we aren't even aware of the expectations. We just do our best." That is an excellent time to ask, "How often does this normally take?" You may find that the reported average is something like five business days. That would make pre-negotiating a starting SLE (Service Level Expectation) of five business days easy. That will allow you to calculate an automatic due date of five days for any record that enters the step you are currently analyzing, and that is far better than what you had. Items that do not stay within those bounds may simply get flagged to help your contributors prioritize them. Still, if the need for further escalation is identified as being warranted in later iterations, the facilities for that will already be in place.

An Agile system will make it easy to change these details later, so experimentation is safe.

10. Who else may need to see the record at this step?

When we ask who else needs to see the record at this step, we're not asking who is responsible for the record at the current step; we are asking who else needs to have visibility into the record at this stage of our process. In our warranty example, the customer's salesperson may want to be aware of any claim as it traverses the entire process. Our finance team may also want to see all "approved" warranty claims that may lead to refund expenses or inventory changes.

11. Is there anything special that needs to happen at this step?

That is a catchall question intended to help a process professional discover anything that may have been missed via the other more focused or targeted questions. Our goal is a deep dive facilitated by asking about any special requirements or edge cases that have not yet been discussed. You want your contributors and stakeholders to access their mental archives, trying to remember the exception cases that may help you catch that last hidden workaround. One of our professionals with more than 20 years of process discovery experience suggests this item must not be overlooked, so plan for it, be okay with the silence while your stakeholders think, and give it the time it deserves.

12. What communication needs to happen at the end of this step?

Remember, we may be defining the endpoint for a simple task or improving the mid-point in a longer-running complex process that spans multiple teams or departments. In the former case, we may only need to notify the requestor that their request has been completed. In the latter case, we may still need to notify our subsequent assignee. We should always consider when to notify the "customer of record" for each request. Again, remember that over-notification will become noise and should be avoided, but critical milestones may be desirable information for our stakeholders.

Additional Data

As a best practice, it is prudent to record who made changes within every step of a process, what they changed, the prior and new values, and when they made the change. In HighGear, this is called the Audit Trail, and HighGear automatically records everything done to a record. Depending on your system, you may need to enable or build such an auditing capability. You may also need to create fields to store the kinds of background metrics or attributes we've discussed. Recording that data as requests, cases, or incidents traverse your process will make performance data easier to record and analyze. For example, you may want to:

1. Record the exact date and time when a record entered the current step of a process.
2. Record the exact date and time that a record left the current step of a process.
3. Record who reported that a step was completed.
4. If you have the Time-in and Time-out date/time stamps, it may be beneficial to do the math and record or display the total time the record lingered within a named step of a process.
5. If your process has routing logic, for example, if the warranty claims clerk has questions that a dealer cannot answer or an end user provided the wrong information, the clerk may send the request back to a previous step (Warranty Request Submission) with a note requesting clarifications. If this type of routing occurs, it would be beneficial to record who sent it back and to track

how many times it traverses this step. These simple but insightful metrics set up a virtuous feedback loop that may help us identify future low-hanging fruit, such as missing data we could have required before a customer or dealer could submit the Order.

Background II – The Psychology of Change

If you are a reader who looks at the table of contents and starts with the section most interesting to you and started here first, please consider reading Part Two, specifically the section on emergent change, before continuing.

It is critical to understand the way change has been organically happening in your organization and how you can leverage and employ those inherent capabilities that are already present within your teams. It is also essential that you understand your teams' existing processes to ensure that you don't confront them unproductively, leading to low adoption. This section will cover several helpful techniques for that cause, but that background will be critical for the diligent agent of change.

Belief precedes action. In other words, what you believe will influence your behaviors and choices. Standford social psychologist Leon Festinger developed and published a widely cited theory of cognitive dissonance. His findings were that when people lived in a way where their beliefs were inconsistent with their actions, a kind of mental stress would arise. Agnostic priests would be an extreme example. Festinger observed that the subjects of his experimentation encountered an urgent internal need to eliminate their "cognitive dissonance" by changing their actions or beliefs.

That is why experienced agents of change understand that if you have not successfully engaged the hearts of your team, you should not yet count on the work of their hands.

With that stated, let's dig in. Consider the excitement the average human being experiences when they discover that things are about to change. Whether an individual or team will easily accept changes often depends on how those impending changes are communicated. Imagine coming into work to be greeted at the door by someone saying, "Did you hear there's going to be big changes?" How everyone will react to that will depend on a variety of signals.

Signal One: Good News or Bad News?

If someone runs up to you with a very concerned look and says, "Did you hear?" what kind of news are you expecting to hear?

If someone walks up to you casually with a big smile, pulls you into a corner, and quietly asks, "Have you heard?" what kind of news are you expecting now?

Let's take that a bit further: if you are about to get on the elevator at work, and someone gets off the elevator and looks unemotional but says nothing and has a box full of their belongings, what do you assume has happened?

The first point we are trying to make here is probably already apparent. Most consider the words we use when we communicate change, but very few consider the method, timing, or tone, and even fewer consider the perspective or disposition of the hearer. Yet, those secondary factors may have more to do with the hearer's interpretation of what you say than the words themselves.

Let's flesh out these examples more to help make the case.

Consider the first example. You have just arrived in the parking lot, and someone runs up to you with a very concerned look and says, "Did you hear?" The truth is that most of us would begin to think about ourselves, whether we would admit it or not. We would wonder if we were about to hear of layoffs. We would wonder if we just got a new boss who is awful. We wonder if this is going to impact our plans for this weekend. The list could go on, but you get the point. But let's imagine that the rest of that sentence goes like this... "Did you hear? We were all supposed to be off today, but Bob never told us! They are painting the buildings today. We all got up, dressed, and came to work this morning for nothing!" That is not the news you were expecting, and it will take your brain a few moments to switch context and process that this is good news because you had probably braced for impact.

Let's unpack our second example: someone walks up to you casually with a big smile, pulls you into a corner, and quietly asks, "Have you heard the robots in HR think a $100 bonus will be enough to make us all feel better about the fact that we have to work through the Thanksgiving weekend this year? What a bunch of losers!" The signals seemed like you were about to receive good news, but now your brain is slowly reprocessing that you've just received bad news. Your emotions are on a roller coaster.

The previous examples underscore that misaligned secondary signaling makes it harder for your hearer to process your message correctly. Let's connect that to organizational change.

"Negative Nancy" (not to be confused with the "Wonderful Nancy" that you know) comes down the hallway with her typically disconcerted facial expressions in full bloom and says to you, "Did you hear that we're getting yet another new system!?" While you may have a history that tells you this Nancy is typically negative, how might that interaction impact your expectations?

Mr. Smart Alec in sales comes down the hallway with a smile on his face and says to you, "Did you hear that the morons in the ivory tower have yet another idea of how we can enter more data into useless systems? Just so you know, the beatings will continue until morale improves!" Alec laughs as he walks away. It's all fun and games for him. Are you more or less excited about the meeting this afternoon to learn about your new information system or process?

All of these things should seem obvious. Perhaps they are Psychology 101. Maybe they are even below that, a remedial class. But if they are apparent, it begs the question, why do so many organizations and leaders fail to consider the impact of information being dripped out through uncontrolled channels?

Signal Two: Helpful or Not?

It is challenging to convince anyone to invest time, talent, or treasure into anything unless they are first convinced they have a problem or opportunity worth addressing.

Consider the example of someone in a first-class seat on a luxury international flight. Let's assume they have just finished a wonderful meal, set the personal air conditioning flow just as they like, pulled the blanket up neck high, and leaned back into their comfortable seat. Would anyone in that position be excited about suddenly being asked to sit upright and put on an uncomfortable backpack? On the other hand, what if the stewardess whispered into their ear that there was a problem with one of the engines, and they wanted everyone in first-class to have one of their top-of-the-line parachutes on, just in case? Now, clearly understanding that there is a significant problem with impending severe risks, the traveling passenger will likely not see themselves as inconvenienced.

This metaphor applies perfectly to a corporate environment. Your teams and leaders have worked very hard to build systems they understand. Even if their systems are a bit archaic or opaque, they have become comfortable with them and how to wield them to accomplish their mission. Perhaps they once complained about all the challenges, but now they have gotten everything situated just as they like. You come along (or maybe you sent an email, or perhaps you've mistakenly allowed Negative Nancy to spread the news for you) and announce that you would like them to jostle themselves out of that comfortable, safe, and relatively productive position to put on a straitjacket (at least that's how they may see it).

Some people in your organization will automatically assume that change will be helpful. They are rare; you should know who they are because they may be your early adopters.

Some people will incorrectly fall into this early adopters category because they are still relatively new and cannot yet see the pain that others have already become accustomed to.

However, your true early adopters are intrinsically motivated by change itself. They are those wonderful people who can't stand stagnant things for too long. They may not be your "Steady Eddies," but they are assets when you need to make a change. We will talk a lot more about identifying, engaging, and leveraging your early adopters, but for now, remember that early adopters will see most change as opportunity.

For everyone else, you must first convince them that their comfortable seat is neither as safe nor as comfortable as they previously believed. You must convince them that the process or system you will ask them to engage solves a previously unseen (or forgotten) risk and will allow them to return to a more significant (and safer) comfort in short order.

This second signal is also about communication. While our first signal was about the approach, this one concerns the problem and solution set. You must convince your stakeholders that the change you will deploy is helpful. You can make a change without completing this, but it will cost you. The time and effort invested in convincing people that a change will benefit them will almost always be a fraction of the time spent recovering from the active and passive resistance you will experience when trying to impose a change upon people not convinced it is in their best interest.

Signal Three: Scary or Safe?

While natural early adopters are less concerned about whether a new change is safe, most others will quickly raise the question of safety. Those mainstream users may not communicate that to you, but they will undoubtedly think about it. They want to hear that putting on our metaphorical backpack does not mean you will soon throw them out of the plane. And, of course, they will also want to know if anyone else has survived when wearing one of these backpacks.

When communicating organizational change, you now have a third component to contemplate. You have ensured you control the method, timing, and tone of communication and that your information is delivered as good news. You are also taking the time to clearly articulate the definitive need and how a failure to act promptly could negatively impact the person about to experience the costs of change. And now, you will also contemplate and explain the efforts and steps you've undertaken to ensure that this change will be safe, or at least as safe as possible. None of us can ever truly ensure that any change is 100% safe. However, we can ensure that we have rapid response mechanisms for the likely exceptions.

Signal Four: Soon?

There's nothing less reassuring than uninformed hyperbole. Making unrealistic claims about how long something will take is never helpful. You've made your communication positive; you've explained why it is needed; you've assured your audience that you will make it safe, and now you must take a deep breath and say, "It will take as long as it takes because we are also committed to getting it right." That doesn't mean that change should take a long time. One of the main pillars of this book is that change generally takes too long and that we should all learn to get it done much faster. However, because there is so little trust in organizational change and the promises that come along with it, it is critical to under-promise and over-deliver.

Remember, you are not making changes so that you can then return to stagnation. You are making changes to get your organization used to being more agile and adopting a new philosophy of frequent and incremental change. Accordingly, credibility will be established or damaged based on your early commitments and delivery. Under-promise and over-deliver.

Your commitment? It will take as long as it takes, and when we are done, it will be excellent!

Signal Five: Proof of Commitment

Imagine standing in a used car lot in front of a late model car with large letters written across the windshield stating, "Sold As Is." Imagine that someone in your family has purchased a vehicle from this dealership before, and the dealer's commitment to stand behind the product was not so great. You're attracted to this model, and the price seems relatively good, but you can't get over that glaring message on the windshield, "Sold As Is." You ask the salesman, "What if I drive this thing for a day or two, and something major goes wrong with the car? What happens then?" When he responds, "Don't worry about it, we'll take care of you!"… do you feel reassured?

Many large organizations have allowed ego-driven Big Bang changes where an organizational leader demands that everyone roll over to the new "brand of the year" system only for leadership to soon change hands. That leaves subordinates behind, saying, "We never should have put that (expletive) system in place." Anyone who has lived through one of those changes is justifiably skeptical when the next big ego states, "This new system is going to be great. You will see! And, whether you like it or not, it's coming!" They are proverbially standing in that used car lot. They may be excited about the new system, just like you may want that model of the car you saw. However, they are not confident that the organization is committed to addressing the unexpected problems that come after a consequential change unless you give them some guarantees.

Organizations that want their people to embrace change must assure their people that they are committed to seeing that change all the way through. The definition of "all the way through" is not "until management feels like we are done." That may get management on board, but that's not enough for a system to succeed. If you want organization-wide engagement and adoption, or even better for everyone to help you accomplish that change successfully… You need to commit that the definition of "done" is when the employees themselves believe that your change has improved the organization AND their jobs. They must have a reason to believe that the project will not be considered complete until their ability to contribute to meaningful customer experiences is graded as an A+.

Many managers will read this and feel daunted. "But it's impossible to get my people to feel like we've ever achieved an A+ with a system rollout." Imagine talking to a friend who wanted to be a baker but was giving up on making cakes. "I've tried repeatedly, but they never come out right!" You would assume this person had followed the directions and added all the ingredients, but what if you found out they hadn't? What if you discovered they skipped the directions or missed at least one critical ingredient? Would you expect their cake to turn out well with no sugar? What if they put the sugar in but forgot the flour?

Organizational change is similar. All the ingredients are required. You cannot leave out one ingredient and expect good results. It just doesn't work that way. If you've never achieved an A+ rated organizational change, it's because you deployed a change to your people versus engaging them to deploy your change, allowing them to see themselves as stakeholders.

If you've never achieved an A+ rated organizational change, it's because you deployed a change to your people versus engaging them to deploy your change, allowing them to see themselves as stakeholders.

The question about commitment is a critical one. Let's go back to our metaphor of the used car lot. Let's change one key piece of the story: you, the person shopping for a used car, own 20% of the dealership. Would you now feel different when the used car salesman says, "Take it home, Susan. If you have any problems, you know we will take care of it."? Of course, you will feel differently in this case. The commitment is more meaningful to you because you are a stakeholder.

If you want your people to believe you are committed to the success of organizational change, don't send them home feeling like consumers. Pull them into the office and remind them that they are stakeholders. Stakeholders have the organization's best interests at heart; they know that the organization is committed to serving them because they are stakeholders. Stakeholders will tell you what they are concerned about, while consumers will lie to you while they shop for a different car. Stakeholders will quickly report problems to you with complete confidence that they will be addressed. Consumers will assume you will leave them hanging. They will go down the hallway with a hostile look, telling other departments how bad it will be.

This concept is relevant and critical for change within a department or team. However, it may not be as practical for deployment across a large organization where hundreds or thousands of users will be affected. That is why our next section is going to be about adoption.

Conclusions on the Psychology of Change

Adoption must happen in stages, but there are more steps to consider in large organizations. In larger groups, you must identify and delight your early adopters with an experience they can brag about. You must identify secondary groups experiencing evident pain who can act as your next round of stakeholders. Those additional stakeholders can then inform the rest of the organization why this change will be helpful, safe, and worthwhile. This kind of positive news will spread as virally as when a terrific car dealership opens up in town and takes care of its customers because it's not what people expect.

It is all about the signals, but it's also going to be about the reinforcement.

Burrhus Frederic Skinner experimented with rats during the late 1920s and 30s. He motivated rats to repetitively complete uninspiring tasks like negotiating a maze via incentives. He placed corn at the maze's center and arranged devices to provide an electric shock whenever a rat went the wrong way.

Skinner posited that negative conditioning and positive reinforcement drove the simple psychology of his rodents. Psychologists seeking to find what motivates people in organizations also looked back on Skinner's work for insights. That may speak poorly of how those organizational psychologists viewed the contributors in a modern enterprise, but the truth is that they get it right, at least partially.

Ultimately, they have shown us that work objectives must be aligned with the rewards and that an organization must also be serious enough about navigating the change to accept the risk of losing some people who don't want to move forward. However, longer-run experiments by Skinner, with his rats, and by organizational designers have also shown that these mechanisms have a shelf life. Implementing positive incentives and disincentives can help us get the team moving in the right direction. Further, the alignment between our stated objectives and how our teams will be rewarded is critical, but these are alignment tools, not long-term management tools. For genuine buy-in, you must achieve *belief*.

Additionally, as noted in our "signals" in various ways, the words and actions of others as we are navigating a change can be powerful allies or enemies to our cause. That is why strong role models are so critical. Just as the acclaimed pediatrician Benjamin Spock regarded role models as key for the favorable development of children, later researchers have found they are just as essential for targeting and developing the behavior of adults. That is why it is so critical that we exclude nay-sayers from our early stages of adoption and recruit positive change agents, creative leaders, and top performers to join our early adoption efforts.

You are going to get this right because you are going to:

- Keep control of the communications about your forthcoming change.
- Ensure that the message is only conveyed by people with a positive attitude.
- Think through all the communication details to ensure that people's expectations are high and that they expect good news and have every reason to believe it.
- Do your research and ensure that you have uncovered a critical problem to thoroughly educate your stakeholders about the risks they face and why it's time to take on change.
- Assure them that it will be safe and that there will be lots of testing.
- Think through and implement incentives and disincentives that align with the desired outcomes.

- Recruit and engage positive role models to join your team of early adopters.
- Tell the masses that by the time they have to work with your new system, there will be a team on standby ready to address any exceptions that arise right away.
- Assure people that you have no intention of making promises you cannot keep. You're going to do everything you can to hit aggressive timelines, but also remind them that you are more committed to rolling out the solutions with care and a commitment to perfection than you are to getting them done quickly or just calling them "done."

Ultimately, you'll be astounded at how much credit everyone else takes for your careful planning. Still, you won't care because those in the know (including you) will know that you did what everybody else believed was impossible. You made organizational change delightful!

The person who believes something is impossible should never interrupt the person doing it.
—Unknown

The greatest of leaders, when he has done it, the people will say, "We have done it ourselves."
—Lao Tsu

It's amazing what you can get done if you don't care who gets the credit.
—Harry Truman

Congratulations! With fresh programming downloaded into your powerful mind, you are ready to show your prowess as a master practitioner in the Psychology of Change!

Background III – It's All About Adoption

There's an old metaphor that we have used for a long time here at HighGear: "One team, one fight, but only one-man rowing." It describes a scenario where a self-proclaimed visionary leader believes that his inspiring speeches have led everyone to engage in his fight with equal enthusiasm. Running out in front of the team with excitement, the leader holds his sword up as he runs towards the enemy, only to realize he is the only one running forward. That is not leadership; it is vulnerability in all the wrong ways.

Critically acclaimed Leadership author John Maxwell said, "If you are leading but no one is following, you're just going on a walk." This metaphor is also salient in process improvement. If you are excited about organizational change but are the only person excited about that organizational change, you are not leading an organizational change at all. You are simply in the inexperienced period between being excited about the change you are leading and telling someone the story about how you got fired in the middle of your grand project. How could that have happened? How could you have been on the cusp of your most significant victory, only to have the rug yanked out from underneath you?

Wisdom comes from experience. Experience comes from making mistakes. Mistakes cost time and money. Accordingly, this "valuable experience" is often left out of executive resumes. The story goes, "I was implementing an exciting new system that would've revolutionized the company, but markets changed, investors got nervous, etc., and they decided to bring someone less visionary in to get the company back to basics until things got better." If you call the Board of Directors at the company that let that executive go, they might tell you the story differently. "Jack had a bold vision, and he got us all excited about it, but one thing after another went wrong. Project timelines and due dates were missed. Budgets were blown. These problems never daunted Jack. He just kept going forward. We were tired of the expenses, the pain, and the frustration we were hearing from the employees, customers, and vendors. Eventually, we no longer believed in the change, but Jack insisted we increase the budget even further. We had to let him go!"

Is it possible that both sides of that story could be true? The answer is yes, and it frequently is. While Jack is a mythical character here, please be assured that the example is based on events unfolding in organizations where strategic change has failed and failed significantly. So, Jack had a vision that exceeded the patience of his stakeholders. The wise person would ask how much patience the company had when Jack started. Did he ever ask? Is the problem that he exceeded their patience, or did he not correctly set their expectations? Did he determine whether his stakeholders were interested in the change? Did he explain the inherent risks if they failed to make this change? Think back to the list we just went through in the previous section. We will probably be able to figure out where Jack's adventure came apart.

If Jack got the job as CEO and got the board to approve a significant budget for him to make substantial change, he would've delivered it as good news! We can probably bet that Jack did an excellent job with signal one. Did Jack convince his stakeholders that the change would help? Maybe. They must've believed it enough to back him, but the question is not about WGTH as much as WBTH.

Wait, what are WGTH and WBTH? As a metaphor, they represent two radio stations, representing the various source types that humans hear from, leading them to make decisions.

WGTH is all good news all the time: What Good Thing Happens?

WBTH is all bad news all the time: What Bad Thing Happens?

Here's the point. If a person or organization decides on an important topic based solely on the input of one of those two stations, you have only done half of your job, and the certainty of follow-through will suffer a corresponding risk.

In Jack's case, Jack may have told the Board of Directors how good things would be if he could get his organizational change completed, but it is doubtful that he told them how bad things would be if he could not get that change completed. How do we know this? Easy: they fired Jack and went back to the status quo. When they began to doubt the path forward, they looked back, like the Israelites contemplating returning to Egypt when the desert turned out to be challenging. "At least in Egypt, we had food!".

It's human nature! When the going gets tough, we are going to doubt the decisions we've made. That is the meaning behind the old saying, "Burn the ships!"

The saying, "burn the ships," comes from *The Mutiny on The Bounty*. In the book (and various movies based on the true story), Capt. Bligh had alienated his crew to the point of mutiny. His crew set him and his loyal officers into a dinghy with limited supplies, leaving them adrift in the ocean. Mr. Christian, the mutineers' leader, and the others who had joined him then sailed to the Pitcairn Islands. They knew they might regret going there if life on the islands became tough. However, having committed mutiny, the price for ever being found on the mainland again would be death. Therefore, they burned the ships in the harbor to cement their commitment. "We are *never* going back to England!"

Let's return to our corporate example. We don't need to analyze the rest of Jack's steps. In his example, roughly based on a true story, we are underscoring the previous section's point that "all the ingredients are necessary to make a satisfactory cake."

If Jack carefully examined his stakeholders, one of the things that may have made a difference here would have been developing a team of early adopters.

Returning to our biblical reference of the Israelites escaping Egypt after crossing the Red Sea and surviving the desert, Moses sent a team of a dozen spies into the promised land. Ten spies returned terrified of the giants they had seen, and two were convinced, in the common vernacular, "We can take 'em!" Two of the Twelve that Moses sent were early adopters. The other Ten probably would have been glad to cross the river into the promised land if the early adopters had returned and told them they'd already safely conquered a city or two, and, boy, those grapes were tasty! That is why early adopters are so critical to organizational change. You will never reach the promised land if you let your nay-sayers lead.

Likewise, if the Board of Directors had already tired of hearing from frustrated stakeholders while Jack myopically pursued his grand vision, we can also be sure of another problem: Jack had frustrated stakeholders.

We could certainly assume that Jack did various things to frustrate his stakeholders. His unreasonable expectations may have been the root cause, or perhaps he selected the wrong vendor to help with the discovery portion of his project. Maybe he or his contractors or subordinate leaders communicated rudely to the team. Perhaps after a long night, he snapped at someone telling him about a problem. ***Or maybe he had selected the wrong stakeholders altogether.***

Early adopters are not just early adopters at work. They are the people who want to have new technology just for the sake of having new technology. They are the young men who can tell you about a new game platform that's only been out for days because they already own it. They are the people who pre-order a new car model after the manufacturer completely redesigns the platform. They are the people who try out a new restaurant the day it opens. They are excited about new technology that may seem useless to others solely because nobody else has it. These early adopters will try new things because trying new things "is cool." They are the sort of people who would go into the promised land and come back convinced, "We can take 'em!"

Does this metaphor really work? Well, how did Moses' story go? After getting agitated with his "resistant people," he and they wandered around in the desert for 40 years with no change. They never made it to the promised land. A later generation with new leadership did. But not Moses nor any of his band of nay-sayers.

If Jack could have identified a group of early adopters from across his supply chain, convinced them to join his beta testing team, and only given them access to the new system in carefully controlled increments, how different might the reports have been to his Board of Directors? "We are hearing that Jack is cooking up some exciting new capabilities down there, but he won't let any of the production teams into it. However, we will approve his hiring additional people for his project team because the customers, vendors, and employees who have seen it are raving about it! It feels like, for the first time in a long time, we will soon be able to pull ahead of our competitors!"

The difference between early adopters, fast followers, and mainstream users is subtle unless you know what you're looking for. We talked a bit about the personality type for early adopters, so let's look at fast followers.

Fast followers are the people who are likely to buy the second year of a popular car model after it has gotten good reviews from early adopters. They don't need to wait until Consumer Reports has five years' worth of data on the car. They want to be ahead of their competitors but don't want to be out on the bleeding edge like the early adopters. Fast followers are willing to take modest risks if they hear that somebody has gotten measurable benefits by engaging with this new option. Fast followers love to ask early adopters lots of questions. Fast followers want to pay attention to trends and jump in on them while they're still new and fresh, but they are also critically evaluating to make sure they don't jump into empty swimming pools and hurt themselves. So, if you want your fast followers to be your second round (in other words, to be the first team you enable to go into full production), you need to make sure that your early adopters have already been delighted, and you need to let them (not you) sell your fast followers. If your early adopters are delighted, the fast followers will likely already be waiting at your door, demanding access by the time you're ready for them.

If your early adopters are unhappy, the last thing you want to do is engage your fast followers. You must delay that step until your early adopters are delighted.

Once your early adopters are delighted and spreading their excitement, you need to consider some additional differences between your early adopters and fast followers. Your early adopters don't care if you have documentation. They are bright, love playing with the coolest new thing, and are more than glad to "figure it out." Your fast followers may be willing to tolerate limited documentation, but they will expect some training, some reference materials, and a decent support system. They will not have the same tolerance for bugs, defects, or "we are figuring it out" responses as your early adopters. You can delight your early adopters with cool stuff. Your fast followers want cool stuff that works well. If you can get that right, your fast followers have significant credibility. Because they blend the courage to take early risks with the well-known risk-mitigating diligence of mainstream users, they can speed your new systems' adoption by helping you create demand for it.

You can talk until you're blue in the face trying to convince a mainstream user to try something new and unproven, and the only thing you will end up with is a blue face. But if you win your early adopters and work through your fast followers, your mainstream users will be waiting at your door demanding access.

We will discuss each of these personalities as we work through the individual implementation steps. Still, if you understand the difference between these personality types, you are already ahead of the curve. Jack didn't understand the difference between these personality types and believed that his position would insulate him from needing to understand or accommodate them. Nothing could have been further from the truth. Successful implementation of processes and technology is as much an art as a science. It is as much follow-through as it is vision. Those who understand these concepts often make change look easy, and those who do not frequently end up like Jack.

Don't be like Jack. Choose your stakeholders carefully. If you want reports of your change to be positive, look for people who are already positive. If you want people to adopt your solution quickly, look for early adopters. If you want to create a groundswell, be willing to do it in stages. If you want to succeed at change, consider changing the people who will help you make it a success. They are as critical as any other part of the process of improvement.

We will soon discuss the critical nature of communication for each stage in our step-by-step guide. Just remember that communications with your early adopters can be more informal. They're excited about being insiders and more than glad to get their updates by the water cooler. Fast followers are going to need some formality. The communication should be regular. They should get a document describing what they are going to experience. They should have clear lines of communication for reporting and resolving problems. They will help you build what you need to attract and delight your mainstream.

Categorize your users correctly and bring them in at the right time, and you will significantly increase your odds of accomplishing what Jack did not.

CHAPTER SIX

10 CRITICAL STEPS FOR LEADERS

The greatest of leaders, when he has done it, the people will say,
"We have done it ourselves."
—Lao Tsu

Step 1. Defining the problem

What needs to change, and WHY?

Sometimes, the things that need to change are apparent. If you come into your office and find a trashcan on fire, you won't have to spend much time convincing people that change is needed. When you direct someone to grab the fire extinguisher, several people will run to do it simultaneously. When you bark out orders that someone should dial 911, it is unlikely that anyone will be offended, and again, you'll have to make sure that you don't have everyone within the sound of your voice calling your first responder at the same time. And the next day, no one will argue when you insist that someone needs to empty the trashcan full of paper more frequently.

Wouldn't it be wonderful if you could expect that same kind of alignment and cooperation when, instead of the trashcan, it is your backside burning? Perhaps that sound of sizzling bacon is the heat you feel coming from the CEO who has just observed the declining performance of your team. Maybe you are feeling it directly from customers telling your employees that they have run out of patience and are switching to another firm. Perhaps you are feeling it from your spouse, who has noticed the decline in your bonuses tied to your department's performance. The fire. The heat. The risks. They are all quite evident to you because you feel them personally. But when your problem is less noticeable to others than a burning trashcan, it can be significantly more challenging to gain the support you need to solve the problem and solve it sustainably.

That is why it is critical to ensure that the problems you discover become as obvious to everyone else as they are to you. They matter to you, and you need to communicate the issues in a way that makes them matter to others. That is why we say step number one must be to define the problem. That may seem counterintuitive if the problem is already apparent to you. However, there are several things that you must keep in mind:

1. What is obvious to you may not be self-evident to others.
2. The impact of not immediately addressing a change may not be clear.
3. The risks presented by a problem are not necessarily resolved by simply resolving the present instance of that problem. In other words, it's not enough just to put out the burning trashcan; you must figure out why it happened and how to ensure it can't happen again. Even if you can put the fire out in the trashcan, having an entire team of specialists quagmire around solving a single high-stakes problem is unproductive. Yet, isn't that what unresolved process problems lead to?

4. When things are less obvious than our proverbial burning trashcan, the "why" must be clearly communicated and *personally connected* to those you need to help you implement and maintain the change.

There are a few key things that your stakeholders, regardless of how wonderful you believe they are, hold above all else. They are:

1. What's in it for me?
2. What's in it for me?
   AND
3. What's in it for me?

If your stakeholder's compensation connects to the number of widgets, units, applications, etc., they complete, but helping you implement your change will reduce that number, even if for just a while, their motivations will be misaligned with your own. They may smile and nod at you while you describe the help you need, but they need to know what is in it for them. You can deny this aspect of human nature but will do so at your peril. A great change manager will leverage this aspect of human nature to their benefit. Your job is not only to define this less visible burning trashcan you have discovered but also to help them understand how their performance will be hindered if this problem is not solved. They need to realize that their job will be at risk if this is not solved. They need to connect the dots to how *their* annual bonus may be impacted or reduced if this problem is not solved. And they also need to know how things will get better for them when the problem is solved.

Defining a problem can be broken down into a few steps:

1. Documentation (Part I): Where do we see the opportunity for improvement?
2. Investigate: Who is responsible for the work in this area?
    a. You will need the input of the stakeholders who receive the outcome.
    b. You must have the input of the leaders or managers who shepherd this work through to that outcome.
    c. You will most likely fail if you don't gather significant input from the contributors who complete the work that leads to that outcome.
3. Measure: Is the problem you're chasing rooted in fact?
    a. Remember, not all reported problems are real. The fact that someone says X is slow does not mean that it is objectively slow.
    b. Is the problem persistent? If you find that a problem is real but rare, determine whether you have some individuals or teams needing additional training. You may have an effective process lacking adequate controls, outside compliance, or inspection regimes. That is an operational problem but not necessarily a process improvement problem.

Pro Tip - Controls: The best process improvement efforts always end with systems that ensure those processes persist and function as designed. Processes implemented without these types of controls have a short shelf life and can harm the long-term credibility of those who implement them.

---

    c. Is this problem worth solving? Not all repeatable or measurable problems are worth the effort. If it takes five people ten days to discuss how to save a low-level employee two minutes per month on a problem with low risk and low impact, it should be evident that there are better uses for a skilled change agent's time. Move on and stop this effort.

4. Benchmark: you must be able to provide proof that better results are possible.

    a. That can come from competitors, so long as it is empirical.

    b. That can come from industry analysts.

    c. That can come from first-hand demonstrations. Consider the ancient proverb we mentioned earlier in the book: The person who believes something is impossible should never interrupt the person doing it. The humor in this saying comes from the idea that naysayers immediately lack credibility in the presence of someone already accomplishing what they have deemed impossible. Leverage that truth.

5. Documentation (Part II): Take the information that you have gathered about the problem, its impacts, its metrics, and its benchmarks and put it together into a clear problem statement.

6. Brainstorm: It's time to build your communication strategy about WHY this problem that you have identified must be addressed now.

    a. Have people who are strong at building compelling messaging help you determine how to connect this problem personally and meaningfully to the stakeholders that can help you resolve it.

b. Have people who are strong at innovation or invention contemplate and draft out the best and easiest means to achieve improved outcomes within the realities you have discovered regarding this problem, the nuances of your organization, and the needs and preferences of your stakeholders. (see Pro Tip Working Genius)

c. Resist the urge to create a finalized or "perfect" plan. Your effort at this early stage is best constrained to simply defining a believable model for how things "could" *realistically* be improved. Your communications will help win the support of the stakeholders, leaders, and contributors you will engage to help you build the plan. That will make it *their plan*, and that is critical.

Pro Tip – Working Genius: Consider having those on your process team take "The Working Genius" assessment. You will only need to invest a very short period for this remarkably effective assessment that helps determine the areas of giftedness for people on your team. The assessment breaks people into six categories:

  i.   Wonder: The person who is naturally curious about a problem.
  ii. Invention: The person who naturally sees and enjoys crafting a new and better way of doing things.
  iii. Discernment: The person with an innate sense of real opportunities versus dead ends or tarpits.
  iv. Galvanizing: The person gifted at and innately enjoys "rallying the troops" around a cause.
  v.   Enabler: The person most likely to volunteer for a new initiative and genuinely support it on an ongoing basis
  vi. Tenacity: The person who enjoys tracking the details of a project and making sure they all get done

On the messaging side, someone gifted in Galvanizing should kick off your effort. That person is not necessarily someone who would grab the bullhorn or think of themselves as a great speaker. It is often the quiet person in the back of the room who will only speak if called upon, but when they do say something, it inspires the resolve of others.

Regarding creating your new "To Be" state, the brainstorming effort for that phase should be led by someone gifted in the area of Invention. Ted Lencioni, the inventor of the "working genius" assessment, has described numerous situations where he has found teams struggling to generate practical new ideas only to realize that none have this "invention" attribute. Avoid the quicksand of trying to improve a process without someone on the team who can look past "the way we do things today" and see "the much easier way we could be doing this."

Perhaps you have both attributes. Fantastic! You may be able to build this problem statement and communication plan on your own. If not, don't hesitate to add someone else to your effort if you only have one and they have the other. If you are neither an inventor nor a galvanizer by nature, please be humble enough to draw one of each (or someone with both attributes) into your effort. When it comes to something this important, where our reputation for making things better is at stake, it is much better to be humble and seek out the help we need than to be humbled by a lack of results when we fail to do so.

7. Documentation (Part III): turn your problem statement and high-level vision for how things could be improved into a document or deck that can be easily presented and distributed to those you will need to bring on board to help accomplish your change. Remember the three key motivations of your audience:
   a. What's in it for me?
   b. What's in it for me?
      AND
   c. What's in it for me?

To address those key concerns, it is critical to connect the dots between your proposed change and how achieving it will personally affect them positively once accomplished or negatively if not accomplished soon.

Remember our two motivational radio station metaphors: WBTH and WGTH.

Ensuring that your problem statement includes messages from both stations is critical.

WBTH: You must help your stakeholders understand what bad things happen (or are often already happening) and how, if they continue, things will get worse for them. For example, you must help them understand how your burning platform (the burning trashcan in our metaphor) may seem like a minor problem now, as they are only annoyed by smoke. Still, it will soon become a critical or existential problem for them. In other words, if we don't put the fire on this burning platform out, the place where we are all employed will crumble into a heap of ashes.

Note: The burning platform metaphor is a staple of change management. It is frequently associated with the "Lean Six Sigma" process improvement methodology but also pre-dates it as an oil-drilling metaphor. The analogy expresses that a small maintenance oil leak on a floating rig may not be considered "the most important thing" by a team that eagerly wants to maximize their oil production and, therefore, their bonuses. However, if the platform they are on (also their temporary home) is on fire because of that "minor maintenance issue," motivations and their outward reflections priorities will quickly get re-sorted.

In other words, If a rescue boat were to come by an oil platform with a minor oil leak and offer everyone the chance to get off the platform and onto the boat, there might be few takers if the more significant risks were not yet clearly understood. However, if that platform were already on fire, it would not be difficult to ask people to leave their temporary home and get on the boat. Just as an oil company's safety office should help its contributors understand the risks, our job is to help our stakeholders understand them and associate them with potential personal pain or benefit BEFORE a broken business process becomes the cause of a broken business.

WGTH: you must help your stakeholders understand what good thing happens (and may already be happening somewhere else) and how a consistent change will make things much better for them, personally. For example, you must help them imagine turning an industry-wide imped-iment into a significant advantage.

In other words, when we address the root cause of this occasional oil leak, the place where our offshore techni-cians are all employed and live will soon be safer and more competitive than others in our market.

Connecting your stakeholders to that outcome person-ally will be easy in some organizations. Suppose you can tie their compensation to organizational performance. In that case, you can draw the line between the potential for improved performance or less frequent distractions and the resulting potential for enhanced compensation. Some audiences will not value or prioritize increased compen-sation. For instance, you may be dealing with a team of professionals that is already highly compensated and may value free time or reduced stress more than additional income. You may also have a younger audience who is more interested in feeling that their work is valuable and has a purpose.

You must consider *your* audience and ensure that you connect the soon-to-be-improved outcomes with the things that make a difference to *them*, not you. You need their help, and you are asking for it because of something that is, if we are honest, in it for you. So, be sure that your plea for help tells them what will be in it for them. Tell them what good thing happens for them once your objective is met.

Now that your problem is well-defined, the WHY (it matters to them) is well documented, a believable draft plan has been crafted, and you have built your advocacy materials, you are ready to start seeking out your change agents.

Step 2. Identifying Process Improvement Contributors

Defining who your contributors are might seem easy. Most would contemplate the "who" regarding who manages or contributes to the flow of work through the process. That is partially correct, but we mean who will be involved in your discovery, testing, communication, early adoption, and training process. That is not a suggestion to gather a group of professionals. Instead, that is your call to identify those stakeholders close enough to the process to help you contemplate the specifics required to ensure your project's success.

- **Discovery:** The people involved in the discovery process should include the process owner and specific key individuals who might handle escalations, exceptions, and errors. That team should also include people who are logical and systematic thinkers. Refer to our pro tip regarding the Working Genius Assessment for potential assistance in identifying these individuals. Your discovery team should include people with the "W" (Wonder) profile as they will be comfortable asking the question, "Why do we do this?" That's important because not everything an organization does deserves to be done. Additionally, the answers given in response to that "why" question will often lead to a greater understanding of the artifacts and information that must be gathered along the way.

  To ensure you don't end up in a rut of simply automating 'the dumb old way you've always done it,' look for people with the "I" (Inventor) profile. These people don't just hear how things are done and accept the premise. Instead, they instinctively ask, "Is that the best way to do it?" Even more critically, they have an innate ability to imagine new and better ways of doing things.

Once you have your discovery team together, turn them loose and let them start doing the discovery. They should ask the questions that lead to a highly detailed understanding of what must be captured as a process flows through your organization and what must be displayed (or made ready to analyze) to ensure the right decisions are made as the work flows through a process. Open-ended questions are best. Binary questions are the worst. In discovery, something that could be answered with a yes or no should be considered an immature question until a thorough understanding of the process has been ascertained.

- **Testing:** The next team you want to assemble is your testing team. These may be the same people you put together for the discovery team. Still, the best testers are detail-oriented people who don't mind repetition and will invest a lot of time in what might seem like uninteresting work to your people with the wonder or inventor attributes. People who are good testers will need to be bright, know that their work matters towards producing an excellent outcome, and have their expectations set correctly. You are not engaging them to test a great new solution; you are engaging them to help prevent a terrible new solution from being delivered.

An excellent testing team will slog through a lot of mud and help you work the kinks out of early concepts. If you don't already have a great testing team, your end users will become the testing team. If they don't believe they signed up for that job, most will be unhappy and likely to tell people that the early experience has been negative. The people they tell will translate that to mean, "the new system is bad." You want to avoid that at all costs, so remember that getting your detail-oriented and highly invested-team of testers together is critical to your success. Tell them how much they matter. Tell them how much their outstanding work will contribute to the future of this new and better process. Why? Because it's true.

A well-tested solution comes out of the gates strong, and that will make a world of difference when you get to the critical phase of end-user adoption.

Now that you have your testing team together, it's time to set them aside. They don't have any work to do until you have early prototypes for them to test. However, you will want to keep them informed about the progress as things go along so that they know what they will be testing. Incorporating their feedback as you go will make them feel highly invested before they even start their work. After all, when they begin their testing, all of their feedback will drive iterative changes to ensure that your ultimate solution is in Shipshape. Why not start with them being confident you have already placed a high value on their feedback by keeping them in the loop as your solution is designed and developed? That brings us to communications...

- **Communications:** Depending on your project's size, your communications team may be just one person. Or, you may need a larger team to develop and deploy the communications as your project progresses. That will depend on your organization and the size of your project. Remember that, as a general rule, you want only as many people involved in a communications effort as are required to ensure the communications are clear and effective. Consider the adage, "None of us are as dumb as all of us." While "many hands" may "make light work," they do not typically make succinct communications nor quick decisions.

If you have had your stakeholders take the working genius test, you will now be looking for folks with the "G" (Galvanizing) attribute. Galvanizers are the people who enjoy and are effective at "rallying the troops." Your communications team's purpose is to keep your various stakeholders informed and solicit their valuable feedback as your process improvement team completes its work. Suppose your project will only take one day (which would suggest you have already read the whole book and mastered the art of agile process improvement). In that case, you may decide that your team leader or project manager (who may be you) can also serve as the communications team for this process improvement effort. Just keep in mind that the goals of your communication team will remain the same whether you have a communications team of one and an audience of one or a large communications team and a large group of stakeholders.

Your communications must be fact-based, time-based, consistent, transparent, and meaningful. Wherever possible, communications should also be in writing. Verbal embellishment is helpful, but it should not be the foundation for those all too critical facts. If the reason for that is not apparent, consider the problem when someone recalls that you promised something would be ready on a specific day when you said it would be ready two weeks later. Your success in turning your deliverable in a week early now looks like a failure because of the subjectivity of a hearer's memory. So the rule of thumb is: Make sure that your communications are in writing and present them verbally whenever possible. Distribute them in written form as a follow-up.

We will provide an example status update in Step 4

- **Early Adoption:** Next, let's briefly discuss early adopters. For the sake of simplicity, let's keep in mind the critical attributes of an early adopter. They:

    1. have acute process- or productivity-related pain
    2. are motivated to engage in positive change
    3. see themselves as stakeholders in your improvement
    4. are generally positive
    5. like to be seen as people who helped bring new ideas and technology into your company

We look for people with "acute pain" because we want individuals and teams with an inherent internal incentive to move forward with us. If our chosen early adopters are unconvinced that their current situation is negative, they will not have the same personal level of motivation to help drive change.

A quick but noteworthy comment: if none of your stakeholders feel acute pain, you are probably working on the wrong process. There are always processes in any organization where someone is miserable with how things get done and the outcomes they produce. If you could find and fix those problems, why work on something no one is convinced is broken?

We included the attribute "they are motivated to engage in positive change" because not everyone is motivated to engage in positive change. That should be intuitive, but it is not. Many process improvers have been surprised to find that someone miserable with how a thing currently works can be made more miserable by engaging them in trying to fix it. Perhaps the reason they are in this state is because they are overwhelmed. Maybe the broken process has been "getting by" because they are doing the work of three people. If you add to that load by demanding that they tell you how to make it better or test early iterations that don't work, or join the "early adopter team" (which is really the 'testing phase 2' team), you may be sinking the person who was barely staying above water. They may be all that is holding your old process together so that your organization can keep running while you get your new process into production.

Certain people are just negative towards change. That's a fact of life that is best accepted. Maybe once you make things better, you will need to determine whether or not they still fit. But that's not today's task. For now, you are on a mission to make your process better. That means you need early adopters! They are the people who wake up in the morning saying, "I'm helping to make things better!" Make sure you have those folks on your team. You're going to need them. They will help catch the few things your testers missed, and they will not get upset about them. They will be excited and eager to tell everyone else in the company how great your new solution is! Please read the section on identifying your early adopters and do the work necessary to get them on board. They will make a world of difference and make you look like a hero. Without them, you may end up looking like a zero.

- **Training:** Our last group, but by no means the least, is our training team. We do not need to run an ad in the newspaper. We do not need to hire a group of contract trainers. These people should be the ones who expressed the E attribute (Enablement) of the Working

Genius test. They are the ones who get on board with a new plan quickly and are willing to help. They will promptly document all the steps your early adopters can show them. Your early adopters have big smiles and are eager to show the great new things they have learned, but they are not that excited about creating a Word document, taking a lot of screenshots, or doing a lot of typing. But your enablement/training team is more than glad to do that. If you need people who can get up in front of a room and present in great detail, you must mix the galvanizers with your enablement folks. Your enablement folks will build the documents, and your galvanizers will convincingly present them as the way to solve the world's problems. However, your enablement folks may be all you need if your training will be mainly one-on-one.

"What are job aids!?" One of our professional services team members once told a client that they would leave them an ample supply of job aids. The generally affable client said, "is this the kind of thing I should see a doctor about?" That was awkward. What we mean by job aids are simple documents that can be printed and taped to the edge of someone's monitor (yes, we know that sounds ancient) so that even soon-to-retire John at the customer service desk has an easy way to recall how he logs into the new system. Job aids should show the most common things in short form.

1. What URL do I use to get to the new system?
2. Do I use the same login I use for the other systems here at work?
3. How do I create a new case?
4. How do I check on the status of a case I submitted previously?

5. How do I see work assigned to me in this new system?
6. How often am I supposed to log in?
7. Will I be notified when someone updates one of my cases in the new system, and how or where will I receive those notifications?

That is just an example list of things to include. You may need to include other items, or you may find some of those unnecessary. Just remember that your goal is not to inform someone with the intellectual curiosity level of your early adopter but to reassure your less adventurous later users that they will be able to find and interact with the system on their own after the training is completed, even if they don't remember everything they were taught.

Your training team should generally use good grammar and have enough of a flair for presentation so that your new system is not branded as ugly by their poor work. Someone who typically takes the time to make their work "look nice" would be ideal. You want to invest a lot of time in your training team. They should be aware of the project from the beginning and be included in all the communications as the project progresses. They need to feel like critical stakeholders and see that their part of the project is coming. Once it is time for them to spring into action, you will need to make them feel extremely comfortable with the new system. It would be advisable to shadow each of them during their first few presentations or training sessions until they proactively say they no longer need that help. Please don't allow them to go out independently until someone intimately familiar with the new solution audits them while they deliver their training.

That's it! You are now aware of the attributes of the people who should be on your various teams and why those attributes matter for the roles you will need them to serve. That's the easy part compared to what comes next. Now you have to go and find them and convince them to help. But again, if you have found a problem causing acute pain, it won't be that hard. And we're confident that you've got this!

Note: Now that you have thought about who should be on your process improvement or change management team, consider having those members download and read Chapter 7.

Chapter 7 focuses on the ten critical steps that must be considered and addressed from the perspective of your team members.

Chapter 7 of this book is available as a free download-able resource from the URL: https://www.TheProcessOf Improvement.com

Step 3. Negotiating the definition of Success

There's a common problem with how management sells ideas to their contributors. To put it simply, they don't! Let's group managers into three process improvement classes for the moment:

Level One: Level One managers have a broken process they want to improve. Everyone knows they are responsible for improving the results, and we can generally assume our managers are hard-working, dedicated, and determined to get those results. While often unaware of the unintended impacts of their management styles, due to limited experience, they may eventually get the needed results. However, the unintended consequences will likely include increased organizational turnover, potentially significant losses of mind share, and negative customer experiences while implementing chaotic changes and abrupt corrections. These level one managers will often convince themselves that these negative transition costs fall into a variety of categories:

A) "These people (stakeholders, contributors, etc.) were never on board anyway!"

While this may be true in some cases, it is equally or more often that people who were once on board fell off board when they saw the chaos begin.

B) "That is collateral damage; they should expect that when I'm making significant changes!"

Significant changes will indeed bring some collateral damage. However, collateral damage can be minimized, mitigated, and communicated promptly so that others can help navigate through unavoidable impacts.

C) "The managers above me didn't realize how hard this would be!"

While this is often true because people get promoted without having learned how to manage change, it's just as often an excuse someone makes when they begin to feel the effects of the chaos they create while leading a disorganized or unruly change.

D) "I don't have enough resources to be successful!"

Scarcity is an ever-present reality. Level one managers don't foresee its unavoidable impacts until they materialize. The answer to this is planning and packing the extra resources likely to be needed when things [will] go wrong.

We could certainly provide a variety of additional examples. Still, the point is that if one has not been through the process of successful change, or been trained, or thoroughly contemplated how to mitigate the risks of sophisticated change, it is likely that the negative impacts of a poorly resources change will lead someone to believe one or more of these untruths. Why? Because it is not human nature to blame ourselves when things go wrong.

The reality is that no manager can efficiently manage change that impacts a team without the buy-in of that team. That's not to say it can't be done. Going around the world will ultimately get you across the street. That doesn't mean that's the way it should be done.

Level Two: Level Two managers have been through unruly changes and recognize the upcoming risks. Concerned about the potential for chaos and its effect on their reputation, they ask for help quickly. They seek their team's buy-in, input, and additional support and resources from their managers, C suite, Board of Directors, etc. The critical point is that they seek that support and those resources before they embark on the change journey. Jim Collins' book "Great by Choice" includes an excellent write-up on the effort to reach the South Pole. It compares the efforts of two competing leaders.

In the true story that Collins unpacks, one leader exercises an iron will and pushes his team to travel light so they can go hard and fast. After all, time is of the essence! The other leader assumes that many things will go wrong and that his team will need to take a more measured pace, enabling them to take significant additional resources to be prepared to address the unexpected. One of the most meaningful takeaways of that riveting story is that reasonable planning and ample resources proved significantly more valuable than high energy, determination, and confidence. When things went wrong, the approach and planning of the latter team not only led to their victory but allowed them to survive the expedition in contrast to the other team.

The level two manager may not have experience or training in leading change management. Still, by gaining access to additional support and resources and attempting to engage their team's buy-in, they are far more likely to be effective and minimize the negative impacts of their change.

Level Three) Level Three managers are either gifted, trained, or heavily experienced in change management. They know that the first thing they must do before planning any change is to define their objectives clearly. That clarity requires well-negotiated, reasonable, and measurable outcomes that all parties have agreed upon.

If you work in a deadline or command-driven organization, you will probably feel nervous at the risk of slowing down the execution of an order to make a plan. The risk is that leadership has already told you what they want, and adding more work to the process will lead to arguments. We are not suggesting you can avoid those arguments. If what leadership hopes to accomplish is not well-negotiated, reasonable, and measurable, those arguments will come anyway. However, if you defer making a solid plan, the arguments will arise after you have already applied significant resources to reach an objective that lacks clarity regarding specific outcomes.

The point is that a level three manager is aware that these individually achievable outcomes must redefine success. Consider the commonly used acronym SMART. That stands for specific, measurable, action-oriented, realistic, and time-based. Just like leaving one ingredient out of a cake, you will not likely get a smart plan if you ignore one of those considerations.

Let's consider how to define these SMART outcomes that increase the odds your change effort will succeed. First of all, please note that a critical requirement is that they are, in fact, "well-negotiated."

Let's assume management says, "It is taking us 90 days to stand up new funds and get them registered. We want you to get that down to 60 days by the end of the year." That sounds like a clear outcome. Technically, it is a clear outcome. However, it's not yet a SMART objective. It is specific. It is measurable. And it is time-based. However, the actions that will enable that outcome are not yet defined. And saying them doesn't assure they are realistic. Until we have addressed these missing elements, we cannot confidently respond, "Got it, boss, I'm on it!"

If your leadership is operating at this third level of management, they would be uninspired by that response and concerned you have little experience in change management.

The correct response to an objective with outcomes that are not yet clear enough to build a plan around would be something like this, "that is certainly a clear objective, and there will be a lot of moving parts for us to consider to ensure that we don't unintentionally break anything while trying to accomplish it. I'd like to quickly study the details, engage the contributors, and see if we can come back to you within a specific time to lay out a plan, a timeline, the actions we will need to take, and how we would communicate that to all our various stakeholders."

If you are in a situation or a company trying to get ahead of competitors or lead the market, this could be a great time to discuss building an incentive plan to reward contributing teams for achieving the effort's goals. However, suppose you are in a situation or a company trying to catch up with competitors or market expectations. In that case, focusing on creating economic incentives might be unwise unless the company is well-resourced to address this change.

Another important environmental factor to consider is the excitement or frustration level of the leader communicating this requested change to you. A frustrated leader will not be excited if they feel they have just communicated an urgent problem and given you a reasonable amount of time, but you respond with something that sounds like you believe the change is impossible. That may leave them with the impression that you want to 'make a plan' to prove that impossibility to them.

That frustrated leader needs to be reassured immediately. Consider crafting a response like, "That is an excellent objective! I'm fully on board and excited that you're allowing me to take on this important challenge! I want to make sure we will be successful, so I'm going to get to work on the details right away and will follow up with you quickly with any concerns, issues, or requests for resources or to see if I can figure out any ways that we might be able to do it sooner and give you the good news!"

That might come across as hyperbole to a leader who is already confident their request is reasonable. In that case, a dryer response might be appropriate. "I understand what you are asking for, and I am bought in on the need. I will engage the right resources on my team, build a plan, and get it back to you quickly to ensure we meet your expectations and agree on the right outcomes."

The reality is that regardless of whether you have an opportunity for flowery communication and the negotiation of bonuses for great contributors who make this happen or whether you are trying to get the proverbial blowtorch off your backside, the critical element remains the same: you must negotiate a clear set of specific, measurable, action-oriented, realistic, and time-based outcomes. Those outcomes are not outcomes that you have simply negotiated with management. Instead, our tactics above, in terms of communication towards your managers or leaders, were intended to buy you time to be the level three leader that effectively engages your contributors. Let's talk about that next.

Engaging your contributors

So, your contributors are working hard to get new funds set up in 90 days. You're about to walk in and tell them the great news that they must figure out how to do the same job with no additional resources in two-thirds of the time. How do you think that's going to go? If you were dreaming of applause, you may be off course. However, if you imagine a room full of blank stares and angry questions coming your way, you're on the right track. That dream you've had of spending your bonus on a vacation to somewhere warm and wonderful is beginning to fade.

So, how can you deliver the tough news while keeping your team motivated and on your side? You start with the "why" you've developed in step one. You communicate that a grave threat is on the horizon, a competitor looking to put you all out of work. Or, perhaps, in the more optimistic scenario, you set a vision of your company being ahead of all the competitors because of innovators like those you have gathered in the room who are always looking to stay one step ahead. Either way, you have described a need for improvement, and your next step is to tell them what part they can contribute and ask them for ideas. The objective you've received from management to reduce 90 days to 60 days doesn't matter right now. You are in 'fact gathering' mode, not 'goal communication' mode, at least not yet. It would be too early for that.

As you get feedback from your team, they will likely start by telling you about things beyond their control that could make things go faster. For instance, they might share something like, "Our legal teams take too long to review the documents we need to put out for new funds. It often takes 6 to 8 weeks even though they only need a day or two to review the documents." Whether using a flip chart, a whiteboard, or just keeping notes on your computer, write that down. You've just found a gold nugget! It may turn out that you could drive 6 to 8 weeks out of your process simply by solving the problem in Legal.

On the other hand, it may turn out that if Legal could turn that around in a week, your team would still need 90 days, so be careful that you don't go to war too quickly with your new weapon until you've tested its effectiveness. That means you will need to meet with the Legal team... But that's for later. For now, you want to know more about how your team thinks they could set these new funds up more quickly.

After giving you a whole series of external factors, if a team feels safe, they may begin to look at things internally. Before continuing, consider an essential factor: Your team needs to feel safe. If they have heard what they think is an unreasonable or unrealistic objective heading their way, they will not feel safe. That's why we haven't gotten to communicating specifics yet. Someone aspiring to be a level three manager would be well advised to read the book "Crucial Conversations," which has a wealth of information about how to deal with challenging conversations and remain effective. One of the critical aspects the book articulates is how to make people feel safe in these crucial conversations so that progress can be made despite the high stakes. The focus is on making sure that someone can listen to understand versus listening to respond (i.e., active listening versus defensive listening). You don't want them in fight or flight mode when you need them to engage their higher intellect.

Let's move on to some of these internal factors. The process stakeholders and contributors you are interviewing may tell you about slow systems. They may advise you regarding process steps they doubt are necessary or producing the intended results. They may discuss requirements management has placed upon them that they are unsure are adding value. You should take copious notes. It would be best if you asked questions like:

- "How long do those things take?"
  - o You should be extremely specific and ask for details about how long each step takes that may not produce value and why they take the time they do.

- o You should ask about alternatives for everything considered of no, low, or unclear value.
- o Those kinds of questions will sound like:
  - "Is there another way we could do what management is looking for here?" or,
  - "Is there a way these steps could be done in parallel?" or,
  - "Is there a way we could get another department to do this for us?" or
  - "If this is mostly the same every time, could we build a template or some sort of automation to accelerate this step?"

All this early discovery aims to get your team thinking about things they believe would be possible if given the time and other resources necessary to implement a beneficial change. Because these are their ideas, you will find it much easier to raise volunteers who will take ownership of implementing those ideas. You will then ask, "How much time do you think you need to get that done?" You can now build a list of things to be invested in to achieve the overall outcome.

Yes, this is a heavy lift! But this is the essential heavy lift. It is the one that will make so much subsequent work lighter. If you have done your research and come up with specific, measurable, action-oriented, realistic, and time-based outcomes along with specific investment requirements (time, talent, and treasure) as well as the outcome-oriented contribution each of these line items could make, you now have the basis of the proposal that you can take back to your leadership.

But leadership just told you to get it done! Yep. You're not going to be excited about going in and telling them that you want to negotiate how you can reach the desired outcomes, but you can do this. When they see that you have done the hard work to make sure that you have those SMART outcomes nailed down, you will either gain their respect right then because of your preparation, or if they decide to ignore your diligence, they will realize it later when the evidence has proven you were right. Yes, this is risky, but it is also how careers are built. You will have everything required to negotiate realistic and probable outcomes from a reasonable and fact-based foundation. Think about it. You have now built your portfolio of potential improvements and categorized and documented their likely costs.

Consider this simple example:

"Dear [leader or leadership team],

I'm so excited about working on your project! I've taken the time to dig in, and the great news is that I believe we can achieve and perhaps even exceed your goals. I have documented several specific incremental outcomes and estimated the resources we need to accomplish each. If you are ready to approve them all, we are prepared to get started immediately. If you only want to approve some of them now, we can defer the other items indefinitely or until we see progress from the lower-hanging fruit.

As item number one, we have found a surprise opportunity. If we have the budget to add two full-time employees to the legal team, we believe we can reduce the time it takes to set up a new fund by four weeks and immediately meet our objective. However, because we want to exceed that goal, I have also inventoried seven other items to help us cut between a few hours and one week from the processing time. We could get 90 to 45 days if we implement all of them. Still, my presentation scheduled for later today, and shared with you here, will be intended to inform you of the projected costs in time and resources needed for each of those items so that you can determine whether or not you deem it to be worthwhile to tackle all of those potential efficiencies or a specific subset."

The frustrated boss will be the hardest to present this to, but if they are rational, they will recognize that you have done your homework and are presenting reality. The forward-looking boss trying to gain an advantage over competitors will be delighted that you have given them exactly what they need to make actual investment-grade decisions. The great news is that if you get approval for everything you have planned, you will not be returning to sell it to your team because your team has already helped you put it together. You have built a realistic and achievable set of outcomes and presented them for approval.

Yes, there will still be more details to dig into. The next step you will take is planning the incremental milestones and getting into the details where further risks and needs will emerge. That's also why you presented your $50,000 budget (that your team thought would be needed to replace an aging system and cut two days out of your process) as a $75,000 budget because something always goes wrong. It isn't that you aren't trying to be lean; you are trying to be realistic.

If your life operates without negative surprises, I recommend you buy a lottery ticket on the way home and throw this book away. If your life functions like the rest of us, leave yourself some breathing room so you don't have to bring constant disappointments back as you work through the details. Set the budgets high enough and expectations low enough that you have room to operate within the reality of Murphy's Law. Set yourself up to bring back unexpected good news when you have either over-performed against your expectations, returned part of the expected budget, or both. Again, this is how great careers are built. And you, as a new level three manager, are about to rise to the top as you take your excited team and begin to plan through the details of making things better.

Step 4. Milestones, metrics, and messaging: Up and down the ladder

It's time! Your leadership team has approved seven out of your ten objectives. They have given you a realistic budget, approved your timeline, and even offered you and your team an exciting incentive plan if you can meet or exceed the objectives and timeline. One part of you is excited! The other part is terrified. Good! You're going to need them both. Your 'excited part' will keep you energized and help you energize your team. The fearful part is going to keep you from making huge mistakes. One of those costly mistakes that many level one managers make is running into big-picture plans without breaking them down into the small and incremental milestones that lead to genuine success.

Remember, you are running a project, and that project is to improve your process. That means you will have to function as a project manager and as a program manager. A project manager works on something with defined starting and ending points. Building a new office building is a project. A program manager organizes and manages the resources necessary to run a program. Filling your office up with people, keeping it fully staffed, and ensuring that those people you hired show up at the right time and do the right things is a process. The successful program manager will break that process into many small processes. Perhaps the one you're working on today (getting funds set up and into the market faster) is just one of the hundreds of things your organization does. But doing it repeatedly whenever a new fund needs to be set up is what makes it a process. Each instance of that process may have a defined start and end, but it is not a project. A project is unlikely to be repeated in its same form. A process may have variations, but it is likely to be repeated in roughly the same form over and over again. Processes can be improved and optimized because of this repetition.

You are now the project manager overseeing the improvement of this process. The elements of your project effort that you will need to treat as or run the way a classical project manager would include:

- defining the milestones of your process improvement
- determining to whom and when you will deliver those milestone reports
- deciding upon the format and medium for those communications

You are also now, at least temporarily, a process owner. You may be improving a process that someone else owns, but don't ever lose sight of the fact that you will be responsible in the short term for any negative or positive changes to the outcomes that the process produces. You can think of yourself as an acting process owner. That means you should understand everything your process owner understands about the process you are working on. However, you need more information because you are getting ready to change that process.

Consider the difference between a physician and a surgeon. One examines a patient; the other makes changes to them. The prep for a physician to walk in and examine a patient is significantly lower than the prep required for a surgeon to walk in and open the patient up. Why? If it isn't apparent, it's because the risks are higher when you're making a change.

In many scenarios, we realize that the process owner and the acting process owner (or person about to perform the surgery on that process) may be the same person. If that is the case, the advice on the additional level of detail you should now try to extract is still appropriate. However, if you are responsible for keeping a process running in its "as is" state, you may want someone else on your team to take over building the "to be" state while you make sure the trains continue to run on time. Likewise, if you have a strong subordinate leader, you may prefer to have them take over running the "as is" state while you take over leading the charge towards your new desired state, i.e., the "to be" state.

But let's get back to the risks. Your patient is on the table. You want your process to wake up feeling a whole lot better. This metaphor works because most changed processes also need critical post-change attention, like when patients wake up after surgery. Likewise, for your process, there will be a post-go-live period where many additional details and elements of nuance will come to light. No amount of planning done at this early stage will prevent the fact that there will be inevitable surprises.

We're giving you the best practices we have learned around planning, but you should never forget that it is a non-negotiable best practice to ensure you have ample resources ready when your new process goes live. That is akin to having a nursing staff prepared, in our surgical metaphor, to help your recovering patient. You should have a very agile system that can be changed quickly based on the feedback you will receive. You should have lots of people ready to accept, process, and implement that feedback as soon as they can do so without creating any unintended side effects. The goal is to clear any late-discovered roadblocks in real-time so that your team can feel the intended benefits of the new systems as quickly as possible.

After a major repair or upgrade, your process will need intensive care until it is fully operational – as defined by its stakeholders. Ignore that need for post-go-live support at the risk of undoing all the hard work you and your team have put in up to this point.

Now that we've addressed the risk, let's talk about how to manage it:

- There will be many big-picture objectives. However, testing is more effective on a smaller scale.
  - o Break significant objectives down into lots of small ones.
  - o Figure out if it's possible to implement those objectives as individual elements.
  - o Build things that depend on or connect to other independent parts wherever possible. If you take this modular approach and one element fails, you only need to repair and test that element rather than the whole system.
- Once large objectives are broken down into small ones, start figuring out which ones can be worked on in parallel.
- Once a list of the items that can be worked on in parallel is built, assign owners.
- To keep things accountable, figure out when these items will need to be completed so that they don't hold up other dependent items that cannot be performed in parallel, and make sure that contributors agree on when those items must and will be done.
  - o Those are two separate items: When must they be done? When will they be done?
- These elements will become your milestones. Take the concepts discussed earlier in this section to heart and add some time as a buffer. Remember Murphy's law, "What can go wrong, will go wrong.

- We should internally publish this list of milestones and beat up on each milestone as a team to ensure it is specific, measurable, action-oriented, realistic, and time-based. Once each item meets that objective in the eyes of your contributors, put a checkmark next to it and call it locked in.
- Once all the objectives have check marks next to them, it's time to publish that list of milestones externally. If you're nervous about these timelines or milestones, add time until you feel better. You may or may not want to share this externally facing list of milestones with your internal team. However, it would be best if you shared this externally. Sharing your list of date-driven milestones creates beneficial nervous energy and organic accountability that will help to keep your process improvement project moving through the mire it will undoubtedly encounter at some point.

The most significant risk in any process improvement effort is not having the elements broken down into individually accomplishable and traceable elements. The second most significant risk is not having those elements organized well enough with clear individual ownership and accountability to include a well-negotiated due date. The third risk is not communicating that organization or accountability in a way that keeps the process transparent and open. You address these risks collectively by breaking significant objectives into small, uniquely accomplishable, clearly owned, and negotiated-deadline-driven objectives. That kind of clear accountability empowers your team to hold itself accountable.

Building and fostering a healthy organizational culture is critical to building a team that holds itself accountable. Culture in the workplace is a hot topic these days, and you'll often find it implemented more in theory than in practice. For more on this concept, consider reading the book "Lessons from the Edge of Business Disaster" and reference the section on culture. Teams supported by great cultures will have a significant advantage in achieving process improvement goals.

But let's go back to the assumption that you have a good culture and your team will hold each other accountable. By publishing that list of milestones to your leadership and other external stakeholders, you are making a confident statement in the form of an open commitment that organically fosters positive accountability. That doesn't mean that things can't go wrong. It does mean that you must also communicate when they do, engaging your customers as stakeholders.

It's time to decide on the specifics of your communication plan. In other words, how often will you update your leadership and external stakeholders? It may not be one size fits all. Perhaps you have a department that will be impacted by some of the changes you will make at milestone three. You may want to keep them on all updates until you reach milestone three. You may have a leadership team that has given you a budget, and perhaps they don't have the time for the weekly updates you've decided to give to your other stakeholders. Maybe once a month is good for them. You will determine whether they get a monthly version of the same report or whether you want someone to generate a summary version for them.

You should consider and document your project's communication plan details beforehand. It would be best to let your audience know why these reports will be meaningful to them and why they should read them. If you have leaders or stakeholders who will not or do not have the time to read those updates, then perhaps you should determine who on your team will make time to stop by or call stakeholders and update them when each of these reports comes out. That is often a critical step or misstep.

An example of a quick periodic update follows:

Today (15 Jan 2026), the team working on the new solution for process X met and made the following decisions:

1. Insufficient data is available to determine how many cases get escalated per week. Therefore, we will allow cases to be escalated manually, run reports on this, and revise the solution 30 days after go-live. We decided to make this easy for the end users by simply giving them a check box to click when they want a case escalated and a text box next to that to enter the reason for escalation. We will include text on the screen to let them know that the audit trail will record who made the escalation and when, along with the information they entered in the text box.

2. The team decided that by deferring the decision and solution development regarding the aforementioned escalation problem, the team could move the project's go-live date forward to February 5th.

3. If you have any concerns regarding these changes or reasons the changes should be reconsidered, please be sure to communicate those to *sally@corpdomain.com* by Thursday, 18 January.

4. The testing team has received a draft prototype of the solution this morning, and another report will be delivered next Monday morning to include the early results from their testing.

5. There are two open issues:
    a. issue number one description
    b. issue number two description

6. This process improvement project is currently on time with no risk of being behind deadline or over budget.

The noteworthy elements of the above update are:

- updates on any decisions recently made
- updates on the current status
- updates on the next steps
- a running list of open issues or concerns
- a general statement on the health or risk level of the project (Color coding or links to supporting data and dashboards are helpful if you can support that in your environment)

Finally, on the topic of communications, consider tone. If a project has suddenly shifted to risky, overdue, or possibly going over budget, your stakeholders responsible for the outcomes may feel fear, sadness, or even fury when they read the update. Make sure the people on your communications team are thoughtful communicators. Taking the extra time to detail why a project has become "at risk" and including information about everything the team is proactively doing to get the process back on track will help significantly. In addition, and as mentioned above, this is one of those times when verbal communication is vital.

If you know a stakeholder is likely to be personally or negatively impacted by a communication about going out, make sure someone on the communication team talks to them personally. Let the email come out as a follow-up to that conversation.

Good news can also have a negative impact. What!? Really. Suppose you plan to be on vacation the week before a new system will go live. If someone suddenly sends an email telling you that it will go live the week you are on vacation, you will imagine your team running around with their arms waving in the air while your boss remembers that you are taking it easy while they catch the flack. Remember, any change stakeholders haven't already bought into is potentially negative. That's why our sample above included a point of contact for the reader of the update to reach out to with concerns or issues. It's also why we chose the words, "If you have any concerns regarding these changes or reasons the changes should be reconsidered, please be sure to communicate those to…".

Mike Tyson famously said, "Everyone has a plan until they get punched in the mouth!" That reality holds for corporate projects as well. Something big will go wrong. Someone you've counted on to deliver an essential portion of the project will get another job, have a death in the family and need to travel, or one of the hundreds of other things that comes along and throws a wrench into your plans. That is where clear communications may save the day. A manager above you may see your update (and the dilemma it reports) and quickly solve a problem you may have been unable to solve on your own.

At some point, your plan will have its Mike Tyson experience. The familiar adage "roll with the punches" applies here. You won't freak out because you told everyone that risks are coming, and you've engaged them all along as empowered stakeholders who want your process improvement effort to succeed. If needed, you are ready to execute plans B, C, or D or to ask your engaged stakeholders to collaborate to develop plan E quickly.

Step 5. Key risks and potential obstacles: collaborate, strategize, and overcome

Defining risks and obstacles early in your process improvement effort will often make the difference between a successful change initiative and one that will become a spectacle for all the wrong reasons.

That warning may cause the eager leader or change management facilitator to hunker down alone in a back room, determined to identify all potential risks or obstacles with the slightest chance of arising. That couldn't be more off-course. The key to successfully defining risks and obstacles is to engage the people about to be affected by the change. They are not used to being asked why they are not excited about forthcoming changes. If they can tell that you are requesting their input from a genuine perspective, they will likely want to explain their trepidations and concerns to you.

You have an exciting vision for the future! You know how much better things will be once this process has been improved! You are confident it can be done! That's why hearing the truth about their beliefs will be hard. The recipients of your forthcoming change will likely have a more pessimistic vision of the future. They expect this will be another half-baked solution that makes their jobs more difficult. They expect the people who drop this new hot mess on them will thoroughly believe that everything will improve this time. Therefore, they rightly worry that you will be frustrated with them for not being able to produce the expected results despite the fresh quagmire you soon aim to deliver.

You may see their default reaction as negativity. After all, you haven't yet had a chance to prove yourself. However, remember that those less equipped for success have made similar claims before you. That is why your words sound like a distant echo to them. Those optimistic predecessors also sent very nice emails about "how great it's been working with everyone" just before they announced they had taken another job. In other words, the progenitor of that change escaped just before the wake of their efforts was fully realized. Therefore, those left behind to deal with the mess have now gained a righteous disbelief in anyone promising the greener pastures of "change." You did not create this concern, but you do have to address it. Taking the time to hear their concerns and lessons learned regarding why these prior projects failed will be essential to turning their doubts into faith.

That isn't just about psychology. It's about "going to the Gemba." Your goal in exercising this proven methodology is to gather risks you could not have seen from a distance and to understand the obstacles or potential obstacles that only someone familiar with the intricacies of the work could help you see.

As we have already discussed, one of the most significant potential obstacles to successful organizational process improvement is the disbelief of those you will need to embrace your change. Carefully and positively engaging your user community to study their concerns will pave a considerable pathway through your most significant potential obstacle.

Consider the phrase "user adoption." I've heard many a CIO, department head, director, etc., state some variation of the following, "We have implemented solutions like this before, but the problem has always been 'user-adoption.'" I find it interesting that so few have ever considered the profound accuracy of the diagnosis hidden in that simple compound word, user-adoption. In the rearview mirror, many see that they have had this issue. If they had contemplated that their end users would ultimately be the ones who would adopt or reject the solution, not the key stakeholders and managers who were part of the planning team, they would have had a much better shot at success. But what are the true implications of adoption?

Adoption is a word that has significant meaning. Let's step outside the business realm momentarily and contemplate the idea of this borrowed word *adoption*. Adoption, in the more common vernacular, is an act of love, service, self-sacrifice, and an investment made into the life of another human being. I'd suggest reading that sentence again before we move on.

To drive home the point of the analogy, imagine how ineffective the typical modus operandi would be if your company marketing team brainstormed what great publicity it would be if all of your department heads were to adopt a needy child personally. Imagine bringing a large group of those leaders into a room who've probably never considered adoption to tell them: "Great news, you're going to adopt a child! It's going to be great for business. You're going to love it! We're not providing additional resources because we have determined you are up to the job. However, it will still be your fault if it doesn't work out.

Further, you will not be involved in selecting the child as we know what's best. Accordingly, we'll drop the child off at each of your homes tomorrow morning. Please let those unable to come to today's meeting know that they will be experiencing the same joy you are very soon!"

Now, imagine the water cooler talk later that afternoon. Is it positive? Maybe a few will like it. Perhaps a few will be on board. Are the rest just negative people?

Let's come back to the more pragmatic discussion of change. This metaphor raises the question: Aren't these the same emotional forces at work when our users adopt a new solution? We ask them to do extra work to help us test a new solution. Not only that, but we are asking them to do it primarily for the benefit of coworkers who will rely on the information and other outputs that come from our user community's part of the process. We are admitting to them that the transition may be difficult. We know there will be surprises, and we will discover incongruence between how we work today and how we assumed things would work when we designed our new solution. Ultimately, we are doing this because we want our customers (whether internal or external) to experience the outcomes of an improved process. In other words, we are asking people with comfortable lives and their own unique objectives to step outside of that comfort zone in the hopes of some future benefit that will be conveyed primarily to others.

Without question, risk assessment (i.e., determining what could go wrong and how we can get ahead of it) is a valuable discipline and set of best practices for any process improvement effort. However, in the real world, risk identification has largely been completed in the wrong place. Risk assessment is not the work of "experts" to be done in back rooms. When done correctly, risk assessment is based on carefully seeking out the aid, input, and buy-in of your soon-to-be user community.

We included the word "collaborate" in the title of this section because of how critical collaboration is to the success of this crucial phase of your process improvement effort. On your own, you may be able to identify 50 to 60% of potential risks. If you have engaged your user community to determine the remaining 40-50% of possible risks, your users will also be inclined to help you resolve them should they materialize.

To aid in the process of this discovery, let's consider the following sample discovery session:

"I've gathered you all here today because no one knows your work better than you. You are the insiders, and I believe you can help make this a success. Your team has identified obstacles we can fix to improve the outcomes your team is delivering. I can help not because I think I know your work better than you but because I can bring my time, experience, new tools, techniques, technology, and other support resources to aid your process improvement effort. But before we proceed, I want to collaborate with you and understand any risks you foresee or any reasons why you think we could fail. I want to show you what we have learned so far, and I'd like to ask for your genuine collaboration to improve our understanding. I need your help to figure out who or what might make it difficult for us to succeed together, and I want your ideas and help to figure out how we can overcome those obstacles should they arise."

That is a bifurcated effort. On the one hand, you are doing a chessboard assessment (i.e., who are my players, and what are their strengths in the area of change?) and a risk assessment (i.e., what are my potential operational or informational obstacles?).

The kinds of questions you might ask that team would include more specific items like:

- I will present what we have captured as the steps of a workflow that moves through this team. Could you validate those for me and let me know if you see any areas where we have been overly specific or too broad?
  o I'm specifically looking to understand either wholesale errors we have made with what we have captured so far or the exceptions (the things that don't follow the "happy path") that you have seen occur that we may not have accounted for.

- I have been told that you are the team that makes things happen. I have been told that you are the people who care about the outcome of this team's work. I know your plates are already full, and I appreciate your time, so I want to be careful not to waste any of that time as we work through this process.
- Can you help me identify who will likely give us helpful feedback (early adopters or testers) and who you think we should keep off the team until we have perfected our new solution?
  - o That distinction doesn't make users "bad" or "good" users. It is essential to acknowledge that some people are so busy carrying the work through our broken process that they don't have the time to be part of our effort. We need to know who those people are that we need to protect and who we need to protect the process and project from until it is less vulnerable.

Key to the statement above is an authentic commitment to accepting feedback and a clear pathway for communicating it, i.e., "If any of you would like to talk to me privately, my door will be open, or you can email me confidentially."

Your commitment to professional confidentiality is critical to the "chessboard assessment" portion of this Q&A. You are identifying risks and obstacles in the form of people. However, if you appear to be using that data to unfairly influence the careers of people who rarely need to undertake change, you will likely only get good input in this area once. That would be negative because it is often not until the second or third round of questions (after trust has been established) that the most helpful information will emerge.

Regarding the operational and informational flows, you will find that your well-thought-through workflow diagrams will soon look like chickens ran through ink and then across your paper. You will have annotated new risks at every turn, decision block, and action step. You will have discovered that there are people you are counting on who are not good at adopting new technology, even if they want to be good at it. You will discover that some people oppose your change because they wanted someone they consider a friend to get the project you are now working on. You will find out that management's assumption that there are enough people to do X directly conflicts with the belief of those who do X. All these discoveries must be factored into your plan.

The time required to incorporate, contemplate, and address these newly discovered considerations will feel like a slowdown, but consider the old carpenter's adage - "measure twice and cut once."

Your risks should be documented. Your obstacles and potential obstacles should be noted. Your business and economic stakeholders should be advised of those risks, and you should share your written thoughts on overcoming each of them with your early adopter community. You will get additional feedback and may be unable to adopt or incorporate all of it. However, you should carefully consider adding as much as you possibly can.

At the risk of overstating the point, your effort is directed at making this *their project*. You're endeavoring to achieve your first round of adoption by making *the plan* to overcome the risks and obstacles you have found together *their plan*. You are fully engaging them in a plan that will result in them being the "new parents" of your baby system. If you can achieve that, they will pull your project through the inevitability of unexpected obstacles. They will share your frustration at not having foreseen the risks that arise midstream and be far more likely to share your determination to overcome all the risks and obstacles.

You may have thought this section or step would be about best practices or specific methodologies and plans for documenting risks and obstacles. There are a plethora of books and resources you can engage with to learn specific annotation protocols or techniques. Our focus has been on the more urgent matter of ensuring you can find and overcome potential risks and obstacles.

In conclusion, risk assessment done in a back office without the engagement of your user community will result in beautiful documents that only address 50 to 60% of the risks and are of limited value to you, your project, or your career if the project fails. Your project's risks and obstacles are best known by your user community, so carefully engaging and listening to them will give you the greatest chance at success.

Step 6. Agile feedback: When, Where, Why, and How

Step six is about two things:

- Planning for how you will solicit, incorporate, and address agile feedback (Agile feedback is the feedback received in real-time while the project is being completed or deployed)
- Planning for how you will "muscle up" for your go-live process, defining and resourcing the *tiger team* that will rapidly respond to the discovery of problems as real work begins to move through your testing, early adoption, and production platforms.

Tiger team: A team of people with varied but relevant skills organized to work on a specific goal or solve a single problem.

Let's first discuss how we will handle the feedback we expect to receive along the way.

If you fail to plan, you are planning to fail." - Benjamin Franklin.

It would be a shame to solicit the input and buy-in of your various stakeholder and user communities before starting a rollout, only to fail at providing guidance on reporting problems when they arise along the way.

Setting clear expectations regarding how late-arriving feedback will be responded to or addressed is also critical. What you want to communicate to your early adopters is to whom and how the problems they find should be reported. For instance, setting up an email address to which all problem reports should be sent is a simple and easy way to address this. It should not be one person's inbox, especially not a person who already has other jobs. It should be a specific address so that someone can be in "support mode" when checking that inbox. Additionally, it is critical to provide a conceptual SLA (Service Level Agreement) to define how your team will respond to different classes of trouble. Here is an example:

Level 1: All problems determined to be impacting the normal function of the business (i.e., keeping the organizational unit from being able to deliver its expected outcomes) will be prioritized as Level 1. All Level 1 items should be reported via email using the same process as lower-level issues. However, a phone call or text message should also be directed to [Person's Name and Mobile Phone Number] to alert them of an active Level 1 problem. All Level 1 issues that are correctly reported and escalated will be responded to within one business hour and will be continuously worked on by the process improvement team until they have resolved the issue or a usable workaround has been discovered and communicated.

Level 2: Any problem causing frustration or delay to at least five process contributors will be deemed Level 2. That will include issues previously determined to be Level 1, for which the support team identified and communicated a workaround but where the workaround is still causing frustration or delay for at least five process contributors. All Level 2 problem reports will be responded to within four business hours, triaged or diagnosed and treated as a high priority, and given as much attention as is appropriate and available. A satisfactory resolution for a Level 2 problem will either be a configuration change, a code change, or a [additional] workaround that either reduces the impact of the problem to less than five contributors or provides a means to continue working without delay or frustration.

Level 3. All problems determined to be sub-optimal, minor, impacting a small group of users in a limited way, and not causing obstacles or delays to the process's expected outcomes will be Level 3. All Level 3 problem reports will be acknowledged within one business day and assigned to someone on the process team or an appropriate technical resource within three business days if required. Level 3 problems will include items previously identified as Level 2, where a workaround has reduced the impact to meet the definition of Level 3. The support team believes [but cannot guarantee] that it will be able to resolve at least 50% of Level 3 problems within one business week and, as often as possible, will be working to fix all of them within two weeks of the problem report.

⁓

That is just an example meant to give you a concept of communicating a plan for the receipt, triage, and escalation or de-escalation of problem reports. You may be surprised by how well such a policy will be received. Openly stating your intentions for various levels of problem reports will instill confidence that impactful problems that can cause user adoption to fail will be responded to and worked on urgently and promptly. Also noteworthy is that you will have clarified that less impactful issues will not be treated the same way. That will be very helpful when something is only affecting one person, giving you the needed time to determine whether or not the root issue may be a user error. In other words, by committing to what you will escalate, you're also clarifying that not everything deserves emergency-level escalation or attention.

Now that we have talked philosophically about how we should communicate our problem-reporting and escalation strategy, let's also discuss how to ensure we can make it a reality. We do not need the project's most expensive or proficient person to check that problem report inbox. However, we need to ensure that it is checked regularly. That is where identifying someone in the orbit of this new solution who has the time to contribute in this way is critical. That may be a group secretary. If the secretary for this group is too busy, perhaps there is an intern or a relatively new employee who is still in training. You need someone who can check that inbox at least once an hour during the business day. You want them to immediately respond to anything that looks like an emergency (or Level 1 issue) with an acknowledgment and a statement that this is being escalated to the right individuals. If they are not sure something is an emergency, they should have your cell phone number and rapid contact info for anyone critical to resolving problems. They need a briefing on what you mean by Level 2 and Level 3 (assuming you were to follow our example) and how to handle or assign those.

If you're assigning things that should be tracked and completed, then it is time to address that. While we would certainly advocate using HighGear because it can serve as both a process improvement platform and an effective means of tracking the details throughout such an implementation, tracking a list of issues does not require a solution as robust as HighGear. You could use many solutions, from text files or Excel spreadsheets to simple task solutions, commodity bug or issue tracking systems, or one of many low-cost ticketing systems. Regardless of what you select, having these things tracked in a format that is not easily overwritten and remains traceable is vital. You must ensure that, if someone takes the time to report an issue, you can generate traceability and visibility for them to ensure that they continue to value the delivery of that input and feedback throughout your project. You must use that tracking to ensure that the work is completed and remind yourself or your process improvement team to report back to users when that problem has been diagnosed, resolved, and made available. Their continuous feedback will ensure that you have fixed the right problem, kept your user community engaged, and informed them that they remain important to you and your team.

The issues your community has discovered or reported along the way should also be tracked in a master document or report that your team or system can distribute to your stakeholders along the way. You should follow many attorneys' advice to their business clients undertaking risky endeavors: "Disclose early and disclose often." The point is that adequately addressing some of the feedback you receive may cause delays. It may take you a week or two to dig into a problem and discover that a Level 3 issue may become a significant obstacle to your planned deployment date. It is adviseable that your business and economic stakeholders see that risk on their radar as early and often as possible.

That being said, you do not want to spam your business and economic stakeholders. You must determine the right cadence for your organization and consider how long the project will run. Sending monthly reports for a project that will only run for six weeks doesn't make sense. Likewise, sending daily reports for a project that will run for six months will ensure that no one reads the emails beyond the second or third day. Regardless, once you determine your appropriate cadence, ensure that your business and economic stakeholders receive regular updates about the emerging risks and obstacles and the progress made towards delivering workarounds or resolving those risks and obstacles.

The bottom line is this: You want a clear, accessible, and straightforward means for your early adopters and key stakeholders to report problems. It doesn't matter whether they realize something in the middle of the night, try an early version of your new solution and find something confusing, or run into an error message or bug. You want them to know how to report it and to have a clear sense of how quickly your tiger team will respond and work on those trouble reports, as well as how and when they will receive updates. If you achieve those objectives, you will have focused on the right thing.

Step 7. Assembling and training the change-ready team.

Numerous well-researched leadership books, such as Jim Collins' Great by Choice, arrive at a similar conclusion on developing leadership: The most significant resource pool of potential leaders within most organizations are those you find already leading.

Not only is this true, but we can also expand the concept to include people ready to serve as early adopters of your business process change. In other words, they are the people already trying to improve things in their own way. They are sometimes viewed negatively by the regulators of an organization. They are the folks looking for a better way and willing to create workarounds. They are the ones who have created a spreadsheet to calculate something that the existing system doesn't handle well enough. They have high ownership, so they do things like writing the names of cases they are tracking on whiteboards despite no longer being responsible for them. They color code things to show status and whether or not projects are running on time.

As someone who needs a group of change-ready early adopters, you must view these people differently, whom some might see as uncooperative mavericks. That is not a suggestion that you want to get antisocial bad actors and empower them to become your change agents. Instead, you want to consider good-willed people who tend to buck the system and may frustrate the typical 'status quo' manager because those "mavericks" are likely to be helpful to your cause if you can engage them. Why? Because as we have discussed, people want to feel they are a part of change.

People will naturally support the changes they think have incorporated their input and feedback. So, it would help if you got people who see change as a positive. When they see your effort addressing what they saw and reported as apparent problems in the past system, they will feel a personal sense of ownership and be willing to overcome oversights and obstacles that might lead your steady-state employees and managers to complain. Not only will they be willing to help you overcome those obstacles, but they will also take a personal sense of accomplishment for having done it and brag about the value of their input in getting it all done.

Consider that quote from Truman again, "It's amazing what you can get done in life if you don't care who gets the credit." You may have been the one who had the great idea to improve this process. You may be the one who has spent countless hours listening to all the details of what was wrong with the old way things were getting done. You may be the one who has worked through the salt mines trying to find the people who are ready for change. You may be the one who stays up late working on the details to make sure that this new change goes off with as few problems as possible. But you are also one person. If you think you can force or even socialize the adoption of this new system on your own, you are either wrong or the only person we've ever encountered who could pull this off. So, in case you're not that one person, let's focus on the obvious need for a group of champions who feel personal ownership and personal accomplishment and want to tell the rest of the world how great their new system is. The emphasis here is that this is *their* new system.

Your change-ready early adopters may be brought into the process when significant planning has already been done. Still, you will now be breaking down your change into the impacts that will hit individual teams or contributors. Your core change agents will engage these early adopters and tell them their input is critical. They will preview a forthcoming system, but you could never imagine it being successful without their help. They are most certainly going to find something they don't like. They are probably going to suggest things that are not exciting to you. They will probably harp on a few things that aren't as important as they think. Trust me, it will be worth working through these issues with them because you are making it *their* system. They will tell everyone how excellent their system is, and because they are in the trenches with your ultimate cachet of new users, they will have credibility that you never will. By engaging these early adopters in this way, you will set yourself up for organic success.

Let's return to the topic of training your core change agents on how to identify these change-ready early adopters. Your core change agents (the ones who have helped you figure out everything the system will need to do) also need to understand the critical importance of beginning to entice the larger audience in stages. They are indeed the first stage. They have helped you envision something that has not yet existed. They have helped you understand the problems with what did exist. They have helped you plan the delta between those two states and given you feedback on your new process's early drafts or technical implementations. Now, you're asking them to recruit the second stage.

First, you want to remind your core change agents exactly why they have been so helpful. They were smart enough to see the problems in the current state. They are willing to think outside the box. They are capable of envisioning something better. They are creative and capable. Now, you want to turn their thinking to those within their ranks or teams who exhibit the early signs of similar potential. And you want to send them out with the same complementary tone to recruit them.

Remember, competent people are busy people. I have often heard the old line, "If you want to get something done, ask someone busy to do it." The saying rings true because people who need things done turn to those who have proven themselves capable of getting things done, and as a result, those doers find their queues ending up rather full. Remembering that hypothesis about busy people when you select early adopters is important. You're not coming to people with idle hands asking them to help with a quick task. You are coming to busy people, asking them to take on a complicated task to empower less busy people to be more effective in the future.

Therefore, it is vital that you remember the three critical elements of human organizational motivation: What's in it for me? What's in it for me? And the all-important, what's in it for me? That is not to suggest that there is no element of altruism within your typical early adopter. Instead, it is essential to remember that you will have an easier time getting them on board if you can follow through and paint the vision for why this change matters to them. In other words, "If we can make this change, others in the team who are often less productive will be able to get much more done." However, the crucial second part of this communication is, "and, therefore, you will end up free to do more thoughtful work and feel less burdened by carrying regular work through the quagmire of a previously broken legacy system."

Keeping a realistic perspective as you seek your group of early adopters is essential. Not everyone who looks like a potential early adopter will have the time. There may be legitimate reasons, such as planning an upcoming wedding or a parallel assignment you were unaware of. People may also be unwilling to do it for reasons you'll never learn or understand. That is okay. Suppose you drag someone kicking and screaming into this project because they look like someone who will be happy to embrace and champion your change. In that case, I hope the conflict between your expectations and reality becomes evident before the extra workload causes them to feel overwhelmed or discouraged.

Some people who look like early adopters are not ready to take it on. Maybe next year. Some people that look like early adopters are not early adopters. They are just rebels who have been able to keep a positive spin on their unwillingness to conform. Whatever the reason, one-third of the people you approach to ask for this help will turn you down. Let them know that is okay. No is a perfectly good outcome. You want the people who are intrigued by this coming change. That's the attitude you need, and those are the people you want to recruit. You will teach your core change agents to find people like that and gather them into a team.

Now that your core change agents have assembled that team (in the form of a list to include detailed contact information, preferably including real-time communication options for all), it's time for you to plan to engage them as a group. That's what we're going to talk about in step eight.

Step 8. Reinforcing the why: Building the perfect change agent

As you read the heading for step eight, focus on "why." You are leading a change. Change is difficult. Leadership is also difficult. One of the things most often overlooked in leadership is that to be a leader, you must have followers. If someone appointed you as a leader, people would probably follow you from the perspective of "They told me to." But as someone leading a change, you need more than that. You need highly engaged people. You are asking for the margins of their time. You are asking them to be creative, and you're asking for that creativity as an additional output from an already busy person. For this reason, you must help them understand why what you are inviting them to do matters to them and, ultimately, the organization.

It's important to recall that at this stage, you are engaging the people who will ultimately sell the user on adopting your new solution to an old and nagging problem.

- You made a presentation for your core change agents, telling them why this change needed to be made. You told them how inconsistent outcomes were hurting the organization.
- You told them the personal danger they could experience if the organization didn't address the problems.
- You also told them about the personal gains they could experience if the organization overcomes these challenges.
- You reminded the competitive-minded among you that there are indeed competitors in the industry whom you collectively desire to defeat.

- You engaged the protective instincts of those who care for their coworkers by telling them about the inherent risks of inaction.
- For those who see themselves as explorers, you gave them the hope of treading into the territory where no one has gone before.

By carefully articulating why this effort is worthwhile and painting a vision of a potential future state beneficial to each group for the above reasons, you've engaged the hearts and minds of your early adopters. But as we've already stated, you must make this new solution theirs to keep them engaged. As we have also discussed, you'll probably have to make more changes to meaningfully incorporate their input and feedback.

Here's a pro tip: Your core change agents may have already predicted things their teams would find critical or delightful. If it is easy, you may want to hold a few of those things back so that when you get that predictable input at this late stage, you can quickly "surface" that new capability in response to your early adopter's feedback.

Your early adopters are, in a sense, your testing team. You should never call them that. You should call them your early adopters. Even better, come up with a title like Tiger Team, Innovation Team, Groundbreakers, Alpha Team, Trailblazers, Process Improvement Team, etc. Accuracy is not as important as inspiration. You may say, "wait, my team is the process improvement team!" Remember the quote, "It's amazing what you can get done in life if you don't care who gets the credit."

Don't worry. Your managers will know that you were in charge of this change. Let people take the credit. Let them tell everyone that your best ideas were theirs. Rest in good spirits knowing that the loftiest credit is reserved for those rare individuals who have discovered how to empower others to get through change, as navigating change is one of the hardest things an organization must do. So, how important is taking credit if you can succeed at that problematic challenge? If that last sentence offends you, this may be an opportunity for some soul-searching. It is often difficult for people determined to absorb all the credit for positive outcomes to achieve them, especially sustainably.

Step 9. Forecast the change you wish to see.

Let's quickly address the importance of setting a vivid vision. Get a photograph (if that is practical) of your early adopter team. If you can't do that, collect their headshots and put them on a PowerPoint slide together. Blend them in with your core change agents. Don't worry about putting yourself on there. Make that slide a preview of what you will show to others after the project succeeds. If you think the project will take four months, then put a date on the top of that slide four months out. Lay out the top two or three things your project will have changed in terms of outcomes, and title it like a newspaper headline with the photograph of your early adopter team below it.

Widget Inc.'s Customers Rave About Streamlined Experience!

The customer service innovation team onboards customers 20% faster than competitors, with zero errors in the first 30 days of the new system going live!

[Team Photo]

Show this to your team. It may seem cheesy, but human beings need vision. A quote from the book of Proverbs says, "Without vision, the people perish." By giving them something to visualize as the future state where they receive credit for the outcomes they have contributed to, you connect them personally to your "why."

That is an easy step to overlook, so most managers and change agents will. But by connecting your team to the outcomes in advance, you will significantly increase your odds of success. By now, I'm sure you have seen the theme: it's about servant leadership. You are the leader of change. You are the one who had the vision all along. You spotted the problem early. You have recruited and incorporated the best and brightest to make it happen. But ultimately, if your true purpose is the success of the project, then you will find yourself well aligned with the ancient quote from Lao Tsu (Sun Tsu's cousin), "The greatest of leaders, when they have done it, the people will say, 'we have done it ourselves.'"

Step 10. It's Go Time. Show commitment!

We've already talked about the critical importance of distributing your cell phone number and other real-time means of communication. You want to distribute this to everyone on your extended change agent and early adopter teams. You are heading into the final phases of refinement. Soon, your new solution will be going live. It would be best to model the behavior you want from your core change agents and early adopters. You will want them to serve as your extended support teams for the masses when it's 'Go Time.' You will want them to believe that this is their system (and it is true because you have made it their system) and that their success and reputations are connected to the success of this new system. For that reason, they would most certainly now rather get a call in the evening (when someone is running into a newly discovered problem) than find out tomorrow that people were unable to do their work, making the project (*their* project) look like a failure.

By letting people know that you are available 24/7 until this project is a success, you are, in our humble experience, actually reducing the risk that you will be frequently called off-hours. When people encounter difficulties, you will be less likely to be hit with angry eruptions. If someone is trying to get something done in your new system and they run into trouble and know that they have been encouraged to call you at any time, they may contact you late at night. More likely, though, they will realize it's unnecessary, and they can email you and follow up in the morning. However, suppose what they're working on is critical, and they cannot reach anyone. In that case, they are far more likely to get infuriated, send a lengthy email about the challenges this problem is causing, and copy numerous others. You can make your own decisions on this. Still, I'd certainly rather be interrupted for 10 or 15 minutes in the evening to resolve an issue than to lose a significant portion of the following morning doing damage control.

Of course, having to do damage control occasionally is inevitable. Each time you have to enter damage control mode, you put yourself in a situation of rebuilding trust quickly. If you find yourself in that mode too often, you may find yourself in a situation like trying to climb a mountain during an avalanche - the rocks may be moving downhill faster than you can climb. If that happens, you will be expending a tremendous amount of energy with minimal results. It is far better, if possible, to avoid ever getting to that point by ensuring people can reach you at any time.

When new users know they can efficiently and promptly escalate items directly to you, they won't escalate to everyone else. That's why you will also have to predispose yourself to the idea that you will receive a few angry phone calls during your project from people you thought were "on your team." Be ready to weather a few of those calls and escalated response cycles. There is a good chance that those same folks who are angry in the moment will turn out to be your most forceful advocates across time. Why? Because you have built trust by demonstrating a commitment to respond quickly and take appropriate action. Intuitively, we all know how rare and valuable that is, and people react to it, so commit to being accessible and taking action and expect dividends.

Note for leaders regarding Chapter Seven:

Some portions of chapter seven, which begins on the following page, may seem redundant to the leader who has already read chapter six. That is by design. Chapter seven will focus more tightly on similar topics but with the differentiated purpose of informing the change agents regarding the specifics of their objectives. This chapter targets the innovative thinkers you will recruit into your inner circle for a process improvement effort or digital transformation team. Therefore, consider having your change agents read at least this chapter to help facilitate your efforts.

You can download this chapter as a free standalone resource (in PDF or similar formats) from the URL: https://www.TheProcessOfImprovement.com., or via scanning the QR code on the last page of this book.

CHAPTER SEVEN

10 CRITICAL STEPS FOR CHANGE AGENTS

This Chapter (Chapter Seven: 10 Critical Steps for Change Agents) is freely available as an excerpt from *The Process of Improvement*. You may freely download and distribute this chapter (in various electronic forms) from https://www. TheProcessOfImprovement.com, so long as the material is neither modified nor sold.

For those who have already read the rest of this book, several topics in this chapter will resemble those we have already defined for organizational leaders. That is by design. You will be doing many tasks similar to those undertaken by the leader of a process improvement effort, but your role will be to dig deeper into details and specifics.

The leader of a process improvement effort should focus on communicating the why, engaging various stakeholders and stakeholder communities, and providing a clear source of inspiration and a commitment to ongoing support during the change process. Those items focus on facilitating high-level outcomes.

On the other hand, change agents will need to focus on the nuanced specifics like the data input requirements, the artifacts that need to be collected, the distribution and presentation of decision support information or contribution requirements (i.e., the exact bits of work we need some individual or team to do at a specific stage), and the analytics required to see if our incremental changes are leading to the desired outcomes.

You are likely reading this because your organization's leadership has seen innovative potential in you and appointed you as a change agent. We already know you want your part to go smashingly! So, what should you do to facilitate implementing changes that make a difference and last? Here are the key steps to consider.

Step 1. Define process contributors, their roles, and contributions

Core question: Who should help me gather the details needed for my part of this process improvement effort?

Your process or subprocess contributors are the people who do the work you are looking to improve, automate, or streamline. If at all practical or possible, we strongly advise you to engage a subset of these contributors to assist you with your forthcoming detailed discovery work. This part of the guide assumes that you are working on a project for a relatively large team of knowledge workers, engineers, or other intellectual contributors who can assist you with your discovery and subsequent documentation efforts. If that is not the case, and you will be the sole discovery resource, we still believe you will find reviewing our guidance on this step helpful.

Ascertaining who the "contributors" are or "who will need to be involved" might seem easy. Most would contemplate the "who" in terms of the process itself. In other words, let's say our widget or item of work is an "X." It would be typical to think we will need the person who receives an "X" and the person who processes an "X." If there are exceptions, we would probably assume we will also need to include the person who handles/reroutes/decides upon the exception handling for "X."

That's good thinking, but it is not all that we mean. When we say 'define who is involved,' we mean 'who will be involved in the discovery, testing, communication, early adoption, and training for your specific part of the process.' Your efforts leaders have recruited you as a change agent. However, effective change agents know they need to foster high engagement to achieve high adoption, which is the key to success. Your objective is to assemble a list of stakeholders for the part of the process you are examining. They do not need to be process improvement professionals, but they do need to be professional and knowledgeable regarding the process areas you want them to help you examine.

The people involved in your discovery should include the process owner and key contributors. Your team should consist of people who are logical and systematic thinkers. In Chapter 6, we discussed the Working Genius Assessment. Your discovery team should include people with the "W" (Wonder) profile as they are the people who will be comfortable asking the question, "Why do we do this?" That's important because not everything an organization does needs to be done, and this is the time to ask. Additionally, the answers to "why" questions will often lead to a greater understanding of the artifacts and information that must be gathered along the way.

To ensure you don't end up in a rut of simply *automating* the dumb way you've always done something, look for people with the "I" (Inventor) profile. People with this attribute don't just hear about how a thing happens and imagine it being made repeatable but are comfortable asking, "Is that the best way to do it?" They are also natural fountains of new and better ideas.

Be forewarned that these human idea factories often produce great and bad ideas on the same assembly line. That is why it is also a good idea to include someone with the "D" (Discernment) attribute, as they will naturally help you separate those items as your Inventor produces them.

While you need a room filled with talented people, you must ask them to leave their egos outside. Process experts may be offended by people who constantly ask the question, "Why?" Inventors can get their feathers ruffled when someone with the discernment gift says, "But I think that's going to cause more problems than it will solve." And likewise, that person with the eye for what works may want to be in charge, but that is not what you brought them for. All in all, you need to help them see themselves as a team that will share credit. It is advisable to set this as a ground rule: "We are going to fight like hungry dogs in this room until we are confident we all agree. Then, we will go out there and win together and take credit together. Everyone agree?"

In some organizations or processes it may turn out that you are the only one doing discovery, and some of the following remarks on how to prepare your people to do discovery may seem not to apply. You can use these best practices if you are the only one mapping out your process or part of the process. We will work from the assumption that you will empower others to do at least part of your discovery.

Once your discovery team is designated, informed, fully committed, and officially commissioned, turn them loose and let them get started. *They* should ask questions that lead to a highly detailed understanding of what must be captured as the work within a process flows through your organization and what must be displayed (or made ready to analyze) to ensure the right decisions are made. Open-ended questions are best. Binary questions are the worst. In discovery, something that could be answered with a yes or no should be considered an immature question until a thorough understanding of the process has been ascertained.

The next team you want to assemble will be the testing team for your part of the new system or process. These may be a subset of the people you put together for the discovery team. Still, the best testers are detail-oriented people who don't mind repetition and don't mind investing a lot of time in what might seem like uninteresting work to your people who have the wonder or inventor attributes (from the working genius profile). People who are good testers will need to be bright, will need to know that their work matters towards producing an excellent outcome, and will need to have their expectations set correctly. You are not engaging them to test a great new solution; you are engaging them to help prevent a terrible one from being delivered. And while we are on the topic of Working Genius profile types, the "E" (Enablement) attribute will lend itself well to your selection of testers, and a "T" (Tenacity) profile will be a great find to help you manage the testing.

A great testing team will slog through a lot of mud and help you work the kinks out of early concepts. If you don't have a great testing team, then engage your end users to become your testing team. If those end users don't believe they signed up for testing, they will be unhappy and likely tell people that the experience is rough. The people they tell will translate that to mean, "the new system is bad." You want to avoid that at all costs, so remember that getting your detail-oriented and highly invested team of testers together is critical to your success. Tell them how much their great work will contribute to the future of this new and better process. Why? Because it's true. A well-tested solution comes out of the gates strong, and that will make a world of difference when you get to the critical phase of end-user adoption.

Step 2. Provision Real-Time communications

Core question: How will your team quickly communicate and resolve critical issues to keep your contributors and stakeholders engaged?

Few things can negatively impact a team's engagement as effectively as slow responses or poor communications. I worked with a highly successful vice president who often said, "A rapid response is the best response to any problem." His point was not to suggest that a quick phone call would resolve a big problem but would quickly terminate the potential perception that a big problem was being left unaddressed.

Over the years, his frequent quip has proven exceedingly true. There will be problems along the way in any change effort. For example, key stakeholders won't remember critical things after your meeting has ended. If they don't know how to tell you immediately, they may never tell you until that critical detail harms your final deployment. Likewise, if you gather a team to assist with testing proposed changes, and they report a problem but perceive that the problem report goes into a black hole, they will likely disengage. The result? You will not be getting the high-quality input that you need.

Your stakeholders roughly fit into two groups. On the one hand, there are "insiders" who are part of your efforts and will be "in the know" and, therefore, aware of changes as they occur. On the other hand, there is your "audience." Your audience stakeholders will be affected by your new process or solution but will not help to "drive the train." Your communication with and to these groups will be different.

The proven need for real-time collaboration for your "inner team" is why we want to ensure you build instant or near-instant communications into your process improvement effort.

- **Collaboration Software:** If you do not already have a team or work management system that includes collaboration, a quick Internet search for "collaboration software" should yield many options. Your team probably already uses an application in that category (Slack, Teams, etc.). Perhaps you need to set up a private channel within your company's collaboration application. If that is not an option for you, and there are no approved applications you can use for real-time communications, set up an email distribution group at the very least. The point is to ensure that you have created a relatively quick (and, if possible, real-time) means for your process improvement team members to collaborate and ensure that everyone is on the same page.

- **Team-wide inbound:** You also need to ensure that your extended stakeholders (those not on your team or in your inner circle) have an easy-to-use means for reporting or escalating problems, questions, concerns, or late discoveries.

  o That could be an email address (team1@...) or a separate slack channel for your team (not your internal "back channel"), etc.

  o Set clear expectations for how quickly your team will respond to new communications in that "inbox" and communicate those to your team. You should also decide who is responsible for doing that and who will be the alternate if that person is unavailable.

  o Treat all inbound communications as critical until they have been triaged and responded to. Remember, "a rapid response is the best response to any problem."

- **Audience-wide outbound:**
  o **Critical:** Critical issues will impact a large group or make all or some vital part of a system unusable. Critical issues must be addressed with urgency. Contact information should be gathered for all key stakeholders so critical events or changes (outages, impacting errors in a new system, etc.) can be immediately communicated to the appropriate parties. When these critical issues arise, ask someone to pick up the phone and call the key stakeholders. Ask those stakeholders to make others aware of the problem and the active effort to resolve it. Then, ALSO ensure that someone quickly follows up with an email or other real-time communication to the remaining stakeholders.
  o **Non-Critical:** Considering who your changes could impact in advance is instrumental. If possible, gather the email addresses of those audience stakeholders and set up an email forwarder (or some other means of broad communication) to inform them of any non-emergency or limited-impact issues.
  o **Updates:** It's time to decide on the specifics of your communication plan. In other words, how often will you update your audience stakeholders? It may not be one size fits all. Perhaps you have a department that will be impacted by some of the changes you will make at milestone three. You may want to keep them on all updates until you reach milestone three. You may have a leadership team that has given you a budget, and perhaps they don't have the time

for the weekly updates you've decided to give to your other stakeholders. Maybe once a month is good for them. You will determine whether they get a monthly version of the same report or whether you want someone to generate a summary version for them.

You should consider and document your project's communication plan details beforehand. It would be best to let your audience know why these reports will be meaningful to them and why they should read them. If you have leaders or stakeholders who will not or do not have the time to read those updates, then perhaps you should determine who on your team will make time to stop by or call stakeholders and update them when each of these reports comes out. That is often a critical step or misstep.

An example of a quick periodic update follows:

Today (15 Jan 2026), the team working on the new solution for process X met and made the following decisions:

1. Insufficient data is available to determine how many cases get escalated per week. Therefore, we will allow cases to be escalated manually, run reports on this, and revise the solution 30 days after go-live. We decided to make this easy for the end users by simply giving

them a check box to click when they want a case escalated and a text box next to that to enter the reason for escalation. We will include text on the screen to let them know that the audit trail will record who made the escalation and when, along with the information they entered in the text box.

2. The team decided that by deferring the decision and solution development regarding the aforementioned escalation problem, the project could move the go-live date forward to February 5th.

3. If you have any concerns regarding these changes or reasons the changes should be reconsidered, please be sure to communicate those to *sally@corpdomain.com* by Thursday, 18 January.

4. The testing team has received a draft prototype of the solution this morning, and another report will be delivered next Monday morning to include the early results from that testing.

5. There are two open issues:
   a. issue number one description
   b. issue number two description

6. This process improvement project is currently on time with no risk of being behind deadline or over budget.

The noteworthy elements of the above update are:

- updates on any decisions recently made
- updates on the current status
- updates on the next steps
- a running list of open issues or concerns
- a general statement on the health or risk level of the project (Color coding or links to supporting data and dashboards are helpful if you can support that in your environment)

- **Communications Tone:** If your portion of a project has suddenly shifted to risky, overdue, or possibly going over budget, your stakeholders responsible for the outcomes may feel fear, sadness, or even fury when they read the update. Make sure the people on your communications team are thoughtful communicators. Taking the extra time to detail why a project has become "at risk" and including information about everything the team is proactively doing to get it back on track will help significantly. In addition, and as mentioned above, this is one of those times when verbal communication is vital.

  If you know a stakeholder is likely to be personally or negatively impacted by a communication about going out, make sure someone on the communication team talks to them personally. Let the email come out as a follow-up to that conversation.

  Good news can also have a negative impact. What!? Really. Suppose you plan to be on vacation the week before a new system will go live. If someone suddenly sends an email telling you that it will go live the week you are on vacation, you will imagine your team running around with their arms waving in the air while your boss remembers that you are taking it easy while they catch the flack. Remember, any change stakeholders haven't already bought into is potentially negative. That's why our sample above included a point of contact for the reader of the update to reach out to with concerns or issues. It's also why we chose the words, "If you have any concerns regarding these changes or reasons the changes should be reconsidered, please be sure to communicate those to…".

Step 3. Define the high-level current and future states for your target process

Core question: What problem are you trying to solve? How will things improve once fixed? How will those improvements help the contributors and stakeholders you will be engaging?

The leader who asked you to read this chapter (or excerpt from *The Process of Improvement*, if you have downloaded just the excerpt) has probably read the entire book. If so, they have probably also communicated what part of a larger process improvement effort you will address. Hopefully, they have clearly articulated the overall problem, its negative or costly impact on your organization, why it needs to be changed now, and what part they ask you to help address. We also expect they have articulated the future state and how that will help you and your organization.

We are now asking you to do roughly the same thing. Consider the portion of the overall problem you will engage with, then consider how you would answer the core question(s) at the beginning of this step. Anyone impacted by your work must receive a clear statement as to why their inconvenience is worthwhile in light of the future benefit their team will experience and why it will improve their work or lives.

Putting this into a PowerPoint slide or equivalent would be a good idea. Type it on a document and paste it on the wall near your phone. Read it frequently. Memorize it. Be ready to recite it on demand. It would be best to consider this a pre-requisite calling card for all your stakeholder engagements.

Here is a basic example:

- Current State (As-Is):
    o One of our largest competitors has promised investors they can be onboarded and receive dividends within 10 days
    o We pay a slightly higher dividend, but online forums have informed prospective investors that our onboarding process typically takes 60 days
    o Savvy investors realize they would need to stay with us for two years to make up for the roughly two months of lost dividends
    o Therefore, we are signing up fewer savvy investors
    o If this continues, the company could have to cut headcount
    o Our department is currently seen as one of the bottlenecks to being competitive
    o Our team is being assembled to address the specific complexities of regulatory requirements while moving at this accelerated speed
- Future State (To-Be):
    o Tiger teams are working in seven departments simultaneously to enable the SLA of onboarding new investors in three business days
    o Marketing states that our higher dividends and faster onboarding will make us market leaders
    o The company will grow by 20% or more next year due to this competitive advantage
    o Management expects to approve doubling annual bonuses as a result of this strategic win and growth

You may want a more in-depth version for your detail-oriented stakeholders, such as:

- Current State (As-Is):
    - One of our largest competitors has promised investors they can be onboarded and receive dividends within 10 days.
        - We have done independent research and validated that they almost always meet or exceed this commitment.
    - We pay a slightly higher dividend, but online forums have informed prospective investors that our onboarding process typically takes 60 days.
        - We believe our higher dividends would attract more high-quality and savvy investors if we could at least match this onboarding time.
    - Savvy investors realize they would need to stay with us for two years to compensate for the roughly two months of lost dividends.
        - To address this challenge via raising dividends alone, we would have to increase dividends by 10-15% or institute a much higher dividend rate for the first year.
        - Additional costs would likely necessitate reducing staff levels by 8-10%.
        - As a result of our inability to address the near-term expectations of our best prospects, we are signing up fewer savvy investors.

- Sales in the last quarter have declined by more than 18%, and the prior quarter was down by 11%.
- Market research revealed the concerns 60 days ago, which prompted this process improvement effort.

o If this continues, the company could have to cut headcount

- Our CFO believes we will be able to avoid this as long as our project succeeds
- If we fail, the company might have to consider outsourcing our team's work to provide the savings needed to raise dividends.

o Our department is currently viewed as one of the bottlenecks to being competitive.

- Therefore, we would likely be one of the first departments to experience cuts or find our jobs getting outsourced.
- That is not the desire of our management team.

o Our team is being assembled to address the specific complexities of regulatory requirements while moving at this accelerated speed.

- We know we can do this, but not without your help.

- Future State (To-Be):

o Tiger teams are working in seven departments simultaneously to enable the SLA of onboarding new investors in three business days.

- Most teams are already ahead of schedule, and excitement is building that we can turn the corner and surprise our competitors with a market-leading solution to this challenge.
- o Marketing states that our higher dividends and faster onboarding will make us market leaders.
  - Our team will be a critical part of making this happen, and your name has already been in the air as someone who can help us make this happen.
- o Due to this competitive advantage, the company will grow by 20% or more next year.
  - That turns this threat into an opportunity.
  - It will also warrant an increased headcount budget to help handle the additional work, allowing us to bring on more great talent.
- o Management expects to approve doubling annual bonuses due to this strategic win and growth.

If you need to add graphics, charts, graphs, or the competitor's logo to help identify your target, do it. The goal is to connect people to the higher cause instead of just connecting them to more work or incoming work requests. Inspired people work. Overworked people just expire.

Step 4. Define the key obstacles and bottlenecks in the existing "as-is" process.

Core question: What *specifically* needs to change to move our process closer to the requirements or objective outcomes stated in our project's charter?

If mapping out your process is like playing chess, mapping out the obstacles and bottlenecks is more like 3D chess. So, before we head into the pragmatics of discovery, design, documentation, and deployment, let's first examine what we are heading to find.

We are not only trying to determine the typical flow of information related to work; we are also trying to determine the specific obstacles and bottlenecks, such as:

- **Information Obstacles:** Areas where information is not available, incorrect, unreliable, or where upstream stakeholders or contributors haven't provided the data needed for decision support or next steps.
- **Resource Obstacles:** Areas lacking the people, machines, finances, computing, validating, or finishing resources necessary to complete a step or handle some specific part of the process.
- **Human Bottlenecks:** This may be related to the obstacles above because someone who does not have the correct information available may slow down the process while they try to determine what to do. There are also circumstances where someone lacks the training to quickly accomplish a particular step while consistently producing the desired outcome. While you may find areas where you suspect someone is not doing their job, it would be wise to wait to draw that conclusion until you have determined whether or not

there are information or resource obstacles at play. While laziness may cause human bottlenecks occasionally, it is not uncommon to find a competent person withering in the face of broken processes. An effective process improver can often restore them to maximum productivity by quickly resolving those core issues.

- **Opacity obstacles:** Unclear processes lead to unclear results. The difference between a low-, medium-, or high-performance team often comes down to how quickly those teams can process or manage exceptions. In a rigid process, it may be necessary to clarify for employees when a service request does not fit the system's process. You should inform your users when they are authorized to manage the exception outside of the process. In other cases, handling potential exceptions and events inside the process may be critical.

- **Alignment obstacles:** A simple example of an alignment obstacle might be a utility company's new service installation team setting the objective to turn new clients up within 60 days, while the quality control team that approves these installations has created a new quality assurance process expected to take 90 days. Again, you do not need to solve all these problems at this stage. You need to make sure that you identify them. Issues of this type that impact different teams or departments will most often need to be escalated to the leaders of those departments or higher to be solved. However, that is a better problem to run into early. If you have not identified them in the discovery phase, they will undoubtedly surface when you deploy your new system, making your deployment look like a failure.

It is also critical to ensure that you, as a change agent, are aware of and focused on the objective outcomes of the new process. Your job is not simply to discover how your contributors are doing work today but to study it with that three-dimensional view to determine which forces are pushing towards the new objective and should be enhanced and which forces are pushing against it so you can resolve those hindrances.

Let's dig further into these obstacles to provide some examples of the challenges you might find and the information you must capture in this step to help overcome them. We offer several low-tech discovery and data capture tools and examples at the URL: https://www.TheProcessOfImprovement.com., or via scanning the QR code on the last page of this book.

- **Information obstacles:** Here, detail matters. You must gather and inventory all the needed fields of information. That is an opportunity for aggregation or disaggregation, consolidation, and organization.

  For example, you may discover that you have been storing all customer names in a "name" field. But you have already heard that marketing wishes you had separately stored first names so that they could set up automated email notifications to clients that would address them by their first name. So, you will need to disaggregate the name data. Perhaps you would record that the existing system includes the field called "name," but you would add "first name" and "last name" as required data capture fields and "middle initial" as a suggested field for the new system. You don't need to work through how to get that information out of the current system or whether someone will need to do that manually for new records only. That is something that the data experts can work on for you. You simply need to determine that this is an information obstacle that could be resolved by this means.

Another example might be that someone must decide about client investments based on various forms. Still, those forms are in a client information directory that is cumbersome and time-consuming to access. You might record that making those decision-support files directly viewable within your new system would help resolve the information obstacle. You don't have to know how to integrate information systems that way; that is up to the developers or the team who configure your solution in a no-code environment. Again, your job is simply to determine whether this information obstacle can be resolved in this way.

- **Resource obstacles:** You may discover significant bottlenecks in your investment client onboarding process because legal team members must review certain disclosures your prospective client has prepared. As someone focused on the customer service portion of this process, you may wonder if it is your job to try to address this. Good news! It isn't. You're not responsible for whether that bottleneck gets resolved, but you are responsible for identifying and documenting it. By raising that issue as a change agent within your team, you ensure that the information will make it onto the radar of people who may be able to change that or will understand that they may need to modify the objective outcomes if they cannot change that other part of the process. There may be a simple opportunity, like training people in another department to review these documents when they are all in order and only sending the complex exceptions to the legal team. That may work in some organizations and under some regulations, while in others, it will not. At the risk of being redundant, you're not responsible for solving this problem; you are simply responsible for identifying, documenting, and escalating it.

You will gain empathy and trust by listening to the people in the team you are working with about how this obstacle impacts them. It is essential in these scenarios where you cannot guarantee the change will be made that you disclose, "I do not have a magic wand; I only have my pen, but I will use it to its greatest effect."

- **Human bottlenecks:** It is surprisingly common while doing process discovery to realize that part of the problem with the existing system has nothing to do with the existing system. In fact, one of the most common incorrect assumptions made by organizations is that new people who have joined the team have learned how things are done from the people who were already there. Some organizations are excellent at training, but most have more significant gaps than they realize. Effective training is not measured by whether or not that training gets completed, how long it takes, or how frequently it is repeated. Effective training is measured by whether or not the people trained have retained and can apply the information.

Many organizations provide significant training on how systems work. Still, that training often serves people who have not previously done any of the work nor had any experience with the system. In this case, research suggests that the average trainee will only retain 10% to 20% of the information. When they arrive at their new job, freshly trained, they will encounter exceptions they do not know how to resolve. They will look to a coworker for advice, but that coworker may also have retained only 20% of their training. So, they will learn about the organization's many organic workarounds instead of the official system. Some of those were healthy workarounds that dealt with a lack of capability in the prior system. Still, many will be workarounds addressing the fact that people do not know what to do within the system. Unfortunately, they will have learned how to do things that create new obstacles or bottlenecks elsewhere.

When you discover human bottlenecks where correct procedures are not being followed, have not been provided, or are being avoided at the expense of downstream exceptions, you must empathize with the user experience at each stage. Ask for significant detail about what might have made it intuitive for them to know what to do next or how to solve what they view as exceptions within the system. In other words, you should have a good library of questions like, "is there any information that someone else could have included in this record to make it easier for you to solve this problem?" Note that this question format externalizes the root cause of the problem. That makes your user feel safe to give productive suggestions about what could have made their job easier.

The data you gather as responses to those questions will often correlate with information or resource obstacles. You may discover that someone upstream had to hurry through something to meet a quota. When gathering specific information needed for a process's later stages, you may find that data collection should have been made mandatory at an earlier point. You may also find out that everything a user needed was provided, making it even more critical to study why they cannot find or incorporate that information. What you are documenting is a combination of the needed information and resources and any obstacles they had with accessing, analyzing, or leveraging those resources.

- **Opacity obstacles:** "When the leader is clear, everything is clear." -Ken Gosnell. The same can be said for processes. When the process is clear, everything is clear. Managers may have trouble making resource decisions because they cannot see the bottlenecks. Thus, a bank of questions designed to reveal the information managers need can be helpful. Remember the same technique: "What could *someone else* have done differently, and what information could have been provided to you that would help you manage your team and resources more effectively?"

The other side of this equation is that you will be doing discovery work that will often expose where things go off the rails, and people will have to make decisions independently. Wherever possible, it is ideal to gather all the information that could have avoided the problem in the first place and ensure it is at the fingertips of the person who is accomplishing this part of the process. However, there may be exceptions that cannot be easily preconceived. For instance, in a loan approval system that contemplates the ratio of debt to income for a person or company, there will be no effective means for systemic calculation if someone who has recently funded a startup has $10 million in the bank, no debt or credit history, and is simply looking for a $1 million loan to build a new building. Upon quick consideration, one might say, "this is a no-brainer. Loan them the money!" But is that correct? What if the organization has already pledged its assets?

Will that building be worth anything if they don't stay in business?

A traditional underwriting process would address many of these items. However, even if all the needed information conveys, there are still times when someone will need to be able to override the requirement for a specific approval ratio subjectively. Perhaps you could say that any credit analyst should be able to ascertain the creditworthiness of the situation.

While you're discovering and identifying opacity obstacles (where a lack of clarity around problem resolution causes slowdowns), you may decide that your organization wants to contemplate making loans in these exceptional circumstances. However, you want the risk to be tiered. In other words, a credit analyst can approve the exception if the risk is less than $1 million. If the risk is between $1 million and $10 million, you may want an officer of the company to approve the transaction. If the risk exceeds $10 million, you may wish to have a subcommittee of the Board of Directors approve the transaction directly. Suggesting a simple laddered exception management routine like this does not make you responsible for approving those loans; it is simply your proposal to clarify a streamlined path forward where operational opacity emerged.

As another example of an opacity obstacle, an expense report that does not meet predefined criteria can cause significant obstacles and bottlenecks in a large organization. Questions will quickly arise like, "Who should we send this to?" or "Who can approve this amount?" Both questions would seem relatively easy to resolve, but are they?

Should an atypical expense report be escalated to a manager within the finance team who approves other general expenses? Or should it be sent to the manager of the person who submitted the expense report? Is there a specific dollar threshold that should trigger higher escalations? Is getting the person's manager to approve the expense sufficient if the expense does not match one of the year's predefined budget categories?

Over time, the answers to these permutations could become predefined process rules. When a new system goes live, especially when the process is more complicated than an expense report, the system designers likely have not considered all potential exceptions. Therefore, it is incumbent upon the person doing detailed discovery of a process to identify that potential opacity as a bottleneck. That is an opportunity to replace opacity with clarity.

For instance, you could predetermine that any expense not meeting predetermined rules, levels, or categories should be routed to a finance leader who will either be authorized to decide how to handle that particular expense or able to reassign it to someone who is authorized to approve or decline the specific type of exception. As a lightweight first step, you could suggest that any such escalation action should automatically create an exception report that gets auto-routed back to the process improvement team. That would ensure accountability around the exception and that the process improvement team would study the exception later, empowering continuous improvement.

Remember: You do not need to solve all these problems right now. You simply need to identify them.

Step 5. Gather the facts

Core question: What data and artifacts will we (or our new system) need to gather to support subsequent decisions, recordkeeping or regulatory requirements, and metrics or key performance indicators?

Quick considerations:

- **End users** typically offer the most nuanced detail about what can go wrong with individual work transactions as they flow across a company's process.
- **Those who manage the workflow and contributions of others** can typically offer meaningful insights and perspectives into how errors, exceptions, and unexpected nuances get handled.
  - o It is not uncommon for the perspectives of these first two groups to differ. It does not mean that one is correct and the other is wrong. They simply bring you different perspectives on the same data, but they must be reconciled early in your process.
- **Working with management to determine the key metrics and milestones** that must be recorded or observed **is critical**. Building recordation of those metrics and milestones into your process improvement plan will ensure you can leverage management's big-picture expertise in real-time to help you iteratively improve the process once it goes live.
- **Plan more time than you think you need for discovery**, and don't assume that everyone will be on the same page.
- It is vital to **gather as much information as possible** before designing systems.

- Incorporating agility or agile systems that can quickly change is essential because new information will be discovered later. The ultimate test of your discovery will be the deployment of your solution. If your launch state is brittle or hard to change, it may fail when just one or two details are wrong.

Key performance indicators (KPIs) are often inserted into processes as an afterthought. If you want to look like a pro when doing your discovery work, follow Stephen Covey's famous advice, "Begin with the end in mind." If you take the time to determine what key performance indicators your organization already values, that will be a great starting point. You should also ask your various stakeholders what information they wish they had about the process. You may need to prod them to imagine enabling currently impossible things. For instance, perhaps they wish they knew the difference between how long something sat in a queue and how long it took the person to do it. That might give them insight into the backlog. Perhaps today, they can only see how long something takes as an aggregate of both the waiting time and production time. If they could separate those two items, they could gain greater clarity over whether they had slow production or needed more people to do the work.

Don't worry about figuring out how to address the analytics side of this problem yet. If you have the right technology or technologists, this will simply be a subsequent effort to facilitate the recordation, organization, and storage of various data elements for later analysis. Keep it simple at your level and ensure you record data points like the date and time that something enters a queue, the date and time that it gets assigned to someone, the date and time that they start working on it, and the date and times they say they are done.

Assuming you've got a modern system or tools, you should be able to organize and analyze that data at a later point quickly. Your job right now is to make sure you've identified and documented the data and artifacts required to build the dashboards you are probably already starting to imagine.

Capture and Display

The individual contributors within a process have a pretty good sense of the data they need to make decisions. Therefore, they can tell you pretty clearly what they now have that they also must have in their new system and what they wish had been provided for them upstream.

You can think of these as the elements you need to "capture and display." You must ask your various stakeholders, "What data must be captured before an item gets to you so you can do your job quickly and effectively?" We also ask, "How do you need that data presented to you?" We are seeking both summary answers (e.g., "When showing me a list of requests, I need to see X and Y at least.") and detailed information, such as, "When I drill into a specific request, I Must Have, Should Have, Could Have, and Won't Need or have A, B, or C."

This line of questioning is known as the **MoSCoW** model:

Must Have
o
Should Have
Could Have
o
Won't Have

We must ask these same questions again for each type of work or request that will come to our team. We must share this data with people doing upstream discovery, just as people or teams doing downstream discovery should share the same data with us, so we are aware of what we must capture to meet downstream productivity requirements as well.

Here are a few more specific examples:

- Suppose a contributor in our team completes a quality assurance step on every 10th record. Do we need them to attach something, enter data to provide context for their findings, or prove they completed the quality assurance control?
- Will an auditor require information that validates that a client-initiated a request even if it has been entered into our system by an internal employee?

Here are a few of the secondary considerations we need to keep in mind when we determine what we need to capture and display in our part of the overall process:

- Who will we capture this data from?
- To whom do we need to display it, and when will they need it?

High-level workflow diagrams are practical artifacts to help clarify the capture requirements harvested from your discovery sessions. However, nothing, including the best of fact-gathering questions, beats empirical data. If you can build a lightweight system quickly and run it for a while, you will give yourself an edge over everyone who gathers data through subjective means because you will have collected your data objectively. In other words, if you can quickly set up a form or simple recording mechanism for your process contributors to use to track when a thing actually happens (i.e., "We just got another request without the proper signatures") versus designing solutions for perceived problems, volumes or severities, you will be able to validate that you are investing your time and resources wisely.

We've seen it time and time again. Objective data is king, while the very best of subjective data remains just that: subjective.

Step 6. Broaden the Horizon

Core question: How will we address the transactions that don't go as expected?

The discovery completed in step five was primarily oriented around "the happy path." The happy path is a phrase that defines a typical record or transaction traversing a process or organization in an expected fashion. If only life worked that way, we would all be happy, too. That is why it is called the happy path. In reality, we know that a significant portion of any organization's work includes some level of exceptions. In other words, we will receive requests that do not fit our ordinary bounds. We need to be able to deal with those exceptions, but it is nearly impossible to map them all out ahead of time. These kinds of exception pathways can be simple things like someone requesting a service we do not offer. The outcome of that should be fairly obvious. However, what if it's an excellent customer that our company cannot afford to lose asking for something we could do but typically don't?

Exceptions can also be embedded far more deeply into a process. Perhaps in onboarding a new client, we have designed a new process assuming that our new anti-money laundering check will yield a binary answer of yes (they are laundering money, and we cannot open their account) or no (they are not laundering this money). That would be sufficient if that were the end of our process, but what if the person designing that process was unaware that the infrequent "yes" outcome required a report to the authorities? We need to bake in the agility so that someone can handle that exception without breaking our process. We also need, where and whenever possible, to figure out how to work that exception into the process.

At this early stage of discovery, we must extract as many of the "known potential exceptions" from our contributors as possible. Existing transactional records will probably show us many exception types and potential outcomes we must replicate. However, as people are excellent at creating workarounds, we mustn't assume that all exceptions will appear in the traditional system of record. These exceptions may end up found in the miscellaneous notes included in our system of record, and they may also end up recorded in various ancillary mechanisms, such as some manager's spreadsheets. That latter example can be more problematic to find. Therefore, asking questions designed to surface these hidden workarounds is critical.

These organic workarounds will not be at the top of most people's minds. However, if you ask numerous questions about exceptions, you will often find many not typically handled within the system. Keep asking questions until you find out whether they are handled in an ad hoc form or recorded in some "work around system" designed for handling these exception cases. That is where we will often find the limitations of the system or process we are trying to fix, resulting in workarounds. They frequently include emails and an associated (potentially volatile) archive, sticky notes that end up in a file folder, or spreadsheets.

In addition to expanding our discovery, in step six, to include exceptions, we need to consider and record critical or noteworthy events. We've mentioned some of these in step five but want to provide more details about a few examples. For instance:

- **Start and stop events:** This can be as simple for a short transaction as recording when a request was received and completed. For a long-running, multi-departmental, or multidisciplined transaction or process, we may want to record the start and stop times for various events, such as the entry to a team's queue. We may want to record something like the date and exact time a request entered the queue for legal review. We may also want to record when the legal team supervisor assigned the new contract to a paralegal or legal resource. We may wish to record the time that the specific person begins reviewing the contract, and we may want to record other specifics like when they had submitted it back to a stakeholder with questions, when those questions were answered, or when the document was approved or declined. Recording these times will allow us to gather empirical data that will empower us to improve the process over time and based on facts.

- **Intermediate events:** We should take some time to contemplate intermediate events such as a route back, approval of a request, rework, clarification step, etc. In a complex process, we may be unable to ascertain all these possibilities. That is where agility is key. Creating "relief valves" is critical so that an end user does not become stuck in a transaction that requires rework—i.e., building a general utility for assigning something back to someone else with notes that clarify the reason for the exception or intermediate event. You can detail the specifics of an intermediate event, think of it as an individual process, and ask the same questions we've already discussed. What information will this person need to complete their portion of the job? When, where, and from whom will we have gathered it? Etc.

- **Inter-related tasks:** In a manufacturing environment, an order that is received may be for something wholly produced internally by machining from raw materials to finished goods. However, in certain circumstances, external items may need to be procured to complete a final assembly for the customer. That order may roughly follow the same path as an internally produced order. However, that order will fall behind in assembly if someone has not already externally sourced the required (sub)components. That would be an interrelated or parallel task. These kinds of tasks can often be discovered by asking, "Is there anything else we ever need to do to complete one of these orders that doesn't happen in your department?"

- **Alerts:** When transactions fall outside the bounds of "normal," it is advisable to ensure that the system will automatically alert the appropriate individuals or teams. That requires two parts of discovery:

   o **What are "the norms?"** In other words, we need to determine whether this is a constant, variable, contractual, or other form of commitment. For instance, in a manufacturing environment, every order may include a need date when the customer wants to receive it. In a financial services environment, and onboarding process may include an internal SLA (Service Level Agreement or Commitment) regarding how many days it should take (or less) onboarding new client. Assuming that every shipped good will take an average of three days to arrive at a client facility, we could take the need date for that manufacturing order and subtract three days. But if we need that order to be at least 90% complete the prior business day to have any chance of meeting that expectation, then we may want to set up an alert for any order that is not at least 90% complete four business days before the need date.

o **Who needs to know?** Creating alerts is something you should handle carefully and sparingly. First, alerts should only go to people who can directly impact the outcomes. Second, alerts must be judiciously limited to ensure they do not become noise. Determining who needs to know should be as simple as figuring out who can impact a change if something is off course. Just keep in mind that you want to limit these alerts to things worth derailing the daily plans of the person with that influence. You certainly want to save them from losing a critical client, but you don't want to text them every 15 minutes during a critical board meeting about things often resolved by the time they can break free and check on them. For that reason, consider the philosophy of incremental escalation. In other words, as an example, wherever possible and practical, start by alerting someone at a lower level one business day earlier.

- **High-level escalations:** Remember to coordinate with the larger process team regarding who needs to be aware of errors, exceptions, escalations, or other problems that might be arising from the part of the process that you are doing your discovery work on. That is best to coordinate after most (if not all) of your department's process-specific discovery has been completed. That way, you will have an inventory of your internal escalations, and you will be able to ask the overall process champion whether or not those bits of information may need escalation to a higher level and when and how. For instance, you may want a Chief Operations Officer to have a dashboard to show the average SLA success rate, with a drill-in capability to see the exceptions if they are of interest at the time. If 99% of the records are running on time, the COO may have no interest in drilling in. However, if that number falls into the 80s, the COO may be particularly interested in seeing the specific records and analyzing for patterns. Making that information available at the dashboard level will be another way of surfacing the data you have already gathered for your part of the process.

Step 7. Contemplate the Milestones

Core question: How will we measure success?

We've already discussed some of the specific things we will need to record to make milestones, performance, and success more visible, but let's take it a level deeper:

- We need to determine what stages matter
- We need to ascertain how long we believe various parts of the work or process *should* take
- We need to ensure that we have recorded the data necessary to surface our KPI (Key Performance Indicators)
- We need to create (or create mockups of) our alerts and dashboards and present them to our key stakeholders and audience to ensure that we capture and display the information they need.

Determining what matters, or more specifically, what stages matter. We may realize that there are two or three "resistance points" with in a process or sub process. We may recognize that they require and deserve the recordation of additional information to help make exceptions or bottlenecks in these areas visible. For instance, in the course of gaining regulatory approval for building a new multinational natural gas pipeline, we may realize that all land agreements and environmental commitments require an average of forty-five days for legal approval. We may also recognize that drafting the first version of one of these documents or commitments may require thirty days. Suppose we also believe that it takes six months of conversations with a prospective landowner to get to the point where drafting a prospective agreement is appropriate and two more weeks after they've seen the agreement to get the documents signed. In that case, we can add these together and develop several potential "pinch points."

First, we must engage our landowners or regulatory agencies at least nine months before we hope to make a go/no-go decision. But that nine months would assume that everything goes through each stage in the amount of time expected. Therefore, it would be too late to realize we don't have a land agreement one week before making a go/no-go decision. Instead, we need to look at each stage in light of the bigger picture. If it has only taken us four months to reach a verbal agreement with a ranch owner, and it only takes us two weeks to develop the contract, we will now be ten weeks ahead of schedule. However, if it took us seven months to reach a verbal agreement, we would be four weeks behind schedule, and we must pay critical attention to these particular records as they traverse the other parts of the process.

Defining the risk level and critical timelines for various items moving through a process is vital. To surface these elements, we need to record more than just the time a record enters a particular stage of work. Myopically assuming that a 42-day approval for a land agreement meant that we were ahead of schedule would be missing a critical part of the story if we had not received the authorization to develop that land agreement until the seventh month. While we are three days ahead of the typical legal turnaround, we are running out of time to make up the other 27 days by which we are behind schedule. Therefore, when we record the entry and exit into and out of each stage, it is important to consider the risk level (a factor of size, financial considerations, need date, and other relevant data points) and highlight those items for special handling. That might require us to build workflow considerations like, "Escalate all 'at risk' transactions to 'high priority,' and move them to the front of the queue."

We might only need to flag a transaction somehow so it will show up on a management dashboard.

The point here is to build upon the elements we have previously been recording, such as the date and time a record enters or exits any specific stage or sub-portion of a process by adding meaning and context. One part of that exercise is the recordation of "risk level" (or whatever you might decide to call it), and the other part is to ensure that that information is appropriately surfaced (through dashboards, alerts, notifications, or routing into a special handling queue, etc.).

Identifying these kinds of needs will come from asking questions like:

- What problems have resulted when these transactions have not gone as expected?
- Who will need to know if something is running behind?
- Who can escalate transactions that have a higher level of urgency, criticality, or risk?
- What regulations are we subject to where these transactions are concerned?
- Who waits for us to complete our work downstream?
    - o Are our downstream deadlines affected by what we do?
    - o Can downstream deadlines be changed if we fall behind?
        - • If downstream deadlines cannot change, where else can time be made up?

These are just examples of the questions that can help you discover "the bigger picture." We hope that some of this information will come to you along with your project charter. In other words, your management team will likely know the risks they are trying to address and be aware of the information they would like you to capture and present to them for later analysis. However, it is best that you never assume they have either completed that step or been able to provide you with a comprehensive list. Your value will always increase when you discover a previously unseen risk.

What does normal look like? We want to ask copious questions about the expected outcomes our process or subprocess should produce. We want to interrogate the stakeholders who have:

- Requested our work
- Will be impacted by our work
- Will receive our work (both in terms of the next recipient and the final recipient)
- Or who are responsible for our work

We want to know what each group believes is "normal" regarding delivery time, update practices and periodicity, and overall outcomes. We are primarily concerned with the delivery and stage times in this step. Examples of the timeline elements we are trying to capture include:

- How quickly do our requestors expect a response to their new request?
- How quickly do our internal contributors expect to be notified of new requests, and by what means or media?
- How many stages, teams, or departments will the work traverse?
    - Are any stages critical, or could they block other tasks, processes, or overall projects or programs if they fall behind?

- Which, if any, of the stages or milestones will warrant notifications for the stakeholders?
  - o Should these notifications be in real-time or summarized across time?
- What internal resources need critical performance indicator data for any or all of this process or sub process?

These are just examples of the questions we can ask to determine what normal looks like and how we can record the data to show that we are succeeding with or exceeding expectations.

Gathering this data early in the process will allow your designs to incorporate the recordation of the information necessary to quickly surface an atypically positive amount of information to your key stakeholders. Remember, you are building an agile system capable of providing real-time insights that will show you and others how to improve the process iteratively. It is essential not to invest time into capturing details for things that are not important. That is why we preceded this topic by leading you to determine what matters. Once you know something matters, it is hard to gather "too much data."

Organizational blindness is a pervasive challenge in numerous industries, and curing it will make you look like a hero.

Step 8. Plan for the plan to change

Core question: If at first you don't succeed, how quickly can you recover?

In process improvement and systems implementation and deployment it is difficult to get an A+ with the first draft. The first draft you give to your testing team is rough. The first draft you give to your early adopters is less rough. By the time they've helped you polish it, you feel like it's wonderful and ready to go. However, by the time you roll it out to your mainstream end-users it is unlikely that you will receive the warm reception expected. Don't let that slow you down at all!

If you expect a rollout of new technology to go smoothly you probably have an unrealistic expectation. That isn't to say that simple changes, or abstracted changes can't be implemented with minimal impact, it simply to say that the closer you are to core operations the more likely you are to cause instability when you implement a significant change. Instability is typically not well received by mainstream users. However, mainstream users have something in common with all of your prior user groups. They respond well when they are responded to well, and quickly. Likewise, their trust will grow if their feedback can be quickly incorporated into corrective actions that resolve their pain and allow them to quickly get back on track towards experiencing the intended benefits of your new enhancement.

Because it is safe for us to assume that a new deployment will cause some level of instability, it is critical for us to prepare for that in multiple ways:

- Ensure sufficient human and other resources are ready to deliver rapid responses when it is time for "go live."

- Be sure there are clear mechanisms for end-users to report any impacting issues they encounter.
- Take care that your mainstream end-user community has been briefed about the coming change, understands why it was necessary, understands what the expected benefits will be (including to them personally), and above all that they know exactly how, to whom, and specifically by what means to report any of the aforementioned impacting issues.
- Last but not least, in fact probably foremost, I sure that you have selected or built an agile system that can quickly incorporate the feedback you will most certainly receive when you deploy your new system or process.
  - o If your new process is simply a trained procedure, then agility may be as simple as assuring that the first draft of a process manual is delivered via three ring notebooks where pages can be replaced when they are updated.
  - o If your new process is rooted in a technical system, then you must ensure ahead of time that you will be able to rapidly make changes based on feedback. Examples might include:
    - A user running into an unexpected condition (a valid record or transaction that does not fall into preconceived boundaries) must be able to execute a work around within a reasonable amount of time. This may require you to design a workaround in the solution, or accommodate a hybrid solution such as someone temporarily attaching a spreadsheet to a record until a more

sanitized solution can be designed and integrated. You may recoil at the idea of a spreadsheet being attached to a record in your new system, but believe me that is far better than people being convinced that your new system cannot handle the exception in deciding that the spreadsheet should live somewhere outside of your system. People will create workarounds, except that and do everything you can to accommodate them being with in your new system.

- One critical consideration: Determine ahead of time who can make changes to the system and at what levels. Many modern systems will allow you to delegate administrative control or configuration capabilities across various components within a larger process or workflow. If you can allow people who are close to an organization's operations to make changes without impacting other parts of the organizations flow, that will facilitate rapid corrections. Systems that provide audit trails for the configuration of the system will provide exceptional safety and accountability. There are risks in distributing and delegating the ability to change a rapidly evolving system, but in our experience, when correctly mitigated, these risks are significantly smaller and less costly then failed adoptions.

To summarize this section, it is critical to insist on agility being part of the design of any new system whether that's system or process be simply policy-based were technically enforced. Your organization will have to invest time and other costs to achieve that upfront, but the dividends that you will harvest when it is time to deploy your new process or solution will more than make up for the investment. Adoption is the difference between successful deployments and unsuccessful deployments. Agility is the key to adoption. No deployment is perfect. But a rapid response will assuage the concerns of a frustrated user, and a rapid response that includes rapid results and corrections (based on their feedback) will gain trust. Trust is a critical component to adoption, and adoption is a critical component to success. As the success of your project will reflect on you, get ahead of the curve and make sure you build agility into your plan at the start.

Step 9. If at first you seem to succeed, keep going anyway

Core question: Is a grand launch the end of your effort or the start of something bigger?

You've done excellent discovery work. You've considered all the key performance indicators your management team could want. You built a system so agile that all the feedback you've received has enabled you to incorporate that feedback into beneficial changes quickly. And the result? You launched your new system based on a thorough redesign process more than two weeks ago, and despite the first few days being a handful, your user community is now raving about your great new system.

So, is this the end of the road? Do we write down all of the details in case we ever need them on a resume, and go and ask our manager for the next project? Or, is this an opportunity to figure out how to significantly impact our organization more than we had expected?

Process improvement is an art and a science. If you have succeeded at both, you have already proven yourself to be a rare individual. Simply ascertaining the details of a complex process can be a lot of work. It requires significant brainpower. Designing a new and better state in the future involves a lot of creativity and thoughtfulness. But getting it to work requires getting people on board and addressing their various inputs and interests. Accomplishing all of that is a big deal. But it is still just the start.

Once you have accomplished something like this, you could write it all down and call it a success, which would be true. However, it is just a milestone along the way for those "in the know." If you take this success and continue iterating it in a shorter fashion, your success will increase and become harder for competitors to imitate or overtake. Because you have gathered empirical data about your operations performance, you have empowered your organization to study that performance data for yourself, looking for bottlenecks and opportunities that could never have been the scene without access to all of this data. There may be cases where you find you have done such a great job up front that there is little left to improve, but that will be rare. In most cases, once you have 30, 60, or 90 days' worth of empirical data, you will find all sorts of new opportunities for improvement if you take the time to look.

You are not responsible for the overall process or processes of the entire organization. Still, you have become an expert and champion for improvement of the portion of the process you engaged. It is likely that you now know that process as intimately as anyone else in the organization. You know what data you have gathered and have come to understand the meaning behind it. You could assume that the managers for whom you have created these dashboards, notifications, and alerts will take that data and run with it. Perhaps they will call you if they need help, but that would be an assumption. Or, you could be proactive.

Consider the opportunity at hand. While your success may get you pulled into other process improvement efforts, there will likely be pauses. What if you took some of that time and proactively reviewed the state of your prior efforts? What if you were to find additional opportunities for incremental enhancement proactively? Then, you would be moving to the next level of expertise in process improvement. That is where you go from being able to execute a one-time change to where you can make change an ongoing process. If trust is already high, why not leverage it? If people believe your questions will lead to new and better tools, outcomes, or recognition for them, why wouldn't they invest more time when you ask for it?

What we have described is the core of iterative process improvement. It is also called continuous improvement. It's the same thing we do in everyday life. We buy a house because it is the perfect place to live. A few years later, we will probably change something like the deck, the garden, or the kitchen. Why? We now have a better understanding of this new environment, and we have learned where and how we could optimize things. While many organizations aspire to continuous improvement, few achieve it. It is not easily orchestrated from the top down, but it is easily affected from the bottom up.

Earlier in *The Process of Improvement*, we included a brief write-up regarding the phrase "going to the Gemba." Suffice it to say that phrase is about going to where the deed is done to get the best information about how work is completed. If you are embedded within a core process contributing team, and you have already been part of a successful process improvement effort, consider yourself as someone who can positively impact the performance of that organization by looking for the opportunity to repeat the process as often as possible.

The delta between good organizations and great organizations is in the details. While two organizations may be able to on board their clients in three business days, the one who can delight their customers while doing that will still win even though their outcomes are equal from a performance perspective. What's the difference between simply satisfying a customer's expectation and delighting a new customer? It can often be as simple as making something just seem easy. Perhaps it is giving them more access to information about how the process is going in real-time. These are often things that are improved iteratively by studying the data that you gathered during your process improvement effort.

Whether this is the first process improvement effort you have ever participated in or the 30th, if your project has succeeded wildly, you are in an exciting position of opportunity. Therefore, we would highly encourage you not to consider this the end of the process of improving yourself in this regard but just the beginning.

Step 10. Game Day – Going Live in style!

Core question: How can you avoid the typical go-live crises that other organizations experience?

It's part of the modern human experience: You call your [Bank | Insurance Company | Cell Phone Provider | Benefits Company…], and a frustrated customer service person apologizes, "I'm so sorry, but we just got a new system, and I am [waiting for the system to load, unable to find your account, not able to get it to take this request you're giving me, etc.]. The long and short of it is they can't do their job because somebody has just delivered them a "new and improved" way of doing things.

As someone who has put a lot of work into your Discovery, Design, Documentation, and now Deployment (by the way, we call that 4-D process improvement), you want your project and all the work you put into it to be an obvious success. Experience has shown that very few people expect that story we can all relate to above. Most are surprised by it. They believe they have checked every detail so often that nothing can go wrong. The more confident they are in statements like that, the more certain they are to live out the old proverb, "Pride cometh before the fall."

So, what differentiates between a smooth rollout, a not-so-smooth rollout, and an unmitigated disaster? There are three factors:

- Testing
- Staged Adoption and feedback loops
- The provisioning of ample resources by the team that expects problems.

Problems are inevitable. Surprises wouldn't be called surprises if you already expected them. So, the best way to ensure you are not surprised by the certainty of problems is to anticipate their probability. Hopefully, you have already done the testing, staged adoption, and set up feedback loops based on the guidance we have given you in the prior nine steps. So, what's left? It's time to provision the ample resources you need when it's time to go live.

You could have 100 people ready to help the five people who were going to be affected by your new system. That is one part of being well prepared, but it won't do any good unless the five people receiving the new system know how to get a hold of you and your ample team. Therefore, please don't overlook the critical importance of distributing your cell phone number and other real-time means of communication. You want to distribute this to those affected by your rollout.

You may think launching the new system is the end, but it is not. You are heading into the final phases of refinement. Soon, your new solution will go live, and that is when you will receive the most significant amount of feedback you have received at any point so far. Hopefully, it's largely or entirely positive. But anything that your brilliant early adopters were able to figure out that this larger group is struggling with will come to light very quickly.

Because you have your back-channel communication set up, you can leverage that to promptly update your team on problems and opportunities as they arise. If you figure out a better way to explain something to your new and larger user base, share that information quickly so everyone else can use the same language. You don't want five people explaining different ways to do things. The scale of complexity that could result from confusing or contradictory messaging is more than you want to deal with. Unify the messaging as quickly as you can, and ensure that your team escalates anything that causes a critical impact as soon as possible.

Because the people above you have also committed to this project being a success, you can reach them quickly if they are needed. Don't hesitate to do that. Everyone is going to have challenges on go-live day. Don't try to be the person who doesn't ask for any help. Ask for all the help you need and more. The measurement of your success will not be in the eyes of the supervisor that you did or did not call. The true measurement of your success will be in the eyes (and subsequent words) of those impacted by the rollout of your new process or system. Those may be the users, the managers waiting to see things flow through the system, or the clients you hope are not waiting on the phone while a frustrated employee mutters under their breath about not being able to save a record.

It would be wise to model the behavior you want from the people who helped you test all this because they are now your best resources for helping the larger user community. If the masses have issues when it's ' Go Time, ' you will want those insiders to serve as your extended support team. It would be best to have them believe that this is their system (and remind them that is true because you have made it their system) and that their success and reputations are also connected to the new system's success. Make them feel like insiders. Get their managers to clear their schedules on "game day,' and setup a war room. Order pizza. Make coffee. If you don't need much of their time that day, excellent! But if it turns out you do, you want them on standby, ready to rescue that person on the phone with a customer.

You want that employee on the phone with a customer to say, "Do you mind hanging on for just a second? We've just rolled out a new system today, and I'm having trouble saving this record. I've got someone standing right down at the end of my row of cubes who can probably help me get it done. I will just need to place you on hold for a few moments."

Because your contributor has a very positive and well-supported go-live experience (thanks to your thoughtful "go-live planning"), their customer, who is ultimately your customer, will have a positive experience as well.

You may have reacted to the idea that you should share your cell phone with all of your end-users. But think it through. Wouldn't you rather get a call in the evening (when someone is running into a newly discovered problem) than find out the next day that people could not do their work, making the project (*their* project) look like a failure?

By letting people know that you or someone on your core team of process change champions are available 24/7 until this project is a success, you are, in our humble experience, actually reducing the risk that your users will frequently call you off-hours. When people encounter difficulties, they will be less likely to express angry eruptions. If someone is trying to get something done in your new system and runs into trouble, but know that they have been encouraged to call you at any time, they may contact you late at night. More likely, though, they will realize it's unnecessary, and they can email you and follow up in the morning. However, suppose what they're working on is critical, and they cannot reach anyone. In that case, they are far more likely to get infuriated and send a lengthy email about the challenges this problem is causing. They may send it to you and copy numerous others you wish they hadn't copied. You can make your own decisions on this. Still, I'd prefer to be interrupted for 10 or 15 minutes in the evening to resolve an issue than to lose a significant portion of the following morning explaining it and doing damage control.

Having to do a bit of damage control may be inevitable – after all, you are changing things, but keep in mind that each time you have to enter damage control mode, you put yourself in a situation of rebuilding trust. If you find yourself in that mode too often, you may find yourself in a situation like trying to climb a mountain during an avalanche. If that happens, you may be expending a tremendous amount of energy with minimal results. It is far better, if possible, to avoid ever getting to that point by ensuring people can reach you at any time.

When new users know they can efficiently and promptly escalate items directly to someone who can resolve them or help them keep going, they won't escalate those problems to everyone else. That's why you will also have to predispose yourself to the idea that you will receive a few angry phone calls during your go-live from people you may have thought were "on your team." Be ready to weather a few of those calls or escalated response cycles. There is a good chance that those same folks who are angry in the moment will turn out to be your most forceful advocates across time. Why? Because you are building trust by demonstrating a commitment to respond quickly and take appropriate action. Intuitively, we all know how rare and valuable that is, and people react to it, so commit to being accessible and taking action and then expect dividends.

PART FOUR

ESTABLISHING A PROCESS
IMPROVEMENT CENTER
OF EXCELLENCE

What is a "center of excellence?" This section may be redundant for those who work in an organization that already operates a process improvement center of excellence. Nonetheless, even an accomplished professional may be glad to pick up a few of the best practices we have observed and shared here. However, if your organization has neither aspired to nor established a center of excellence, let's start with a clarifying definition.

A center of excellence is a group, team, or practice focused entirely or intermittently on accomplishing a particular task with a high degree of outcome-oriented consistency, repeatability, and professionalism.

The ambiguity between whether any specific center of excellence is a group, a team, or a full-blown "practice" would be determined by whether each engagement of that center of excellence utilizes the same group of people for each project or pulls in a varying team for each. For many organizations, a center of excellence is not about people. Instead, it is a series of disciplines, documents, best practices, and institutional knowledge applied consistently over time to improve processes rapidly and incrementally.

For instance, one of the government organizations we have served has appointed a central person to review and organize process improvement or automation requests. That person routes or escalates requests objectively worthy of management or team attention. That person may also manage and orchestrate the teams involved in any specific process improvement effort. Because of the variety of requests and their sources, the teams employed to implement each change will likely differ.

In other words, a request to improve a process in a purchasing department should not be organized and run without people with expertise in procurement. Likewise, it would be remiss to organize that kind of team without people interacting with the purchasing or procurement process from various perspectives, such as a vendor, requestor, or auditor.

The people within a business or agency may not view those requesting something as stakeholders in their purchasing process, but they are. They are "the internal customer." Vendors are also part of the purchasing process. It may seem hazardous to involve someone outside your organization, whom you might suspect of wanting to arrange your purchasing process to have all orders come to them. However, they can offer significant insight into where the bottlenecks in your process exist.

Standardization of Intake

The disciplines, or best practices, involved in standing up a center of excellence start with "intake." You must standardize the format for submitting requests for process improvement resources. Your early "standard" will undoubtedly evolve, but at a minimum, you need the following information for any request you will receive in your new center of excellence:

- What department or business process is identified as having a problem worthy of solution?
- If resources are required, is there a budget? How much, and who has the authority to allocate it, if needed?
- Who are the recommended internal subject matter experts (SMEs), external stakeholders, or champions of change you should engage for this requested process improvement effort?
- A brief description of the problem.
- A brief description of the impacts caused by that problem.
- A description of how many workers, departments, or outside stakeholders are impacted when the problem occurs.
- An estimate of how often this problem occurs.
- An estimate of the cost of this problem.
  - o That should be as simple as a formula taking the impact of the problem and its cost multiplied by the frequency (i.e., Cost x Frequency = Cost).
  - o A simple paragraph or formula justifying how the stated cost per impact was assessed
- When work on this problem could begin (are the stakeholders and SMEs available?)

- Are there any blackout periods when this work could not be completed – (e.g., "We cannot make any changes to our system during the fourth quarter.")
- Does this potential improvement align with any high-level corporate objectives? If so, which ones and how? That technique is often referred to as "cascaded goals alignment."

Standardizing incoming requests for a center of excellence allows you to score them for comparison. Not all requests a center of excellence receives will be worth the time needed to address them. Problems that occur infrequently or only affect one person but might take a year to change may not be a beneficial use of time. If, on the other hand, you might be able to solve a problem in one month or less, that would immediately save three person-months per year, that would appear to be the better investment. However, that doesn't mean that it should be the priority. Suppose your organization has decided that sales must be increased by 10% in order for the company to stay in business, and you have a request that would take three months to complete and increase sales by 5%. That should take precedence over the shorter project because of its alignment with the overall corporate objectives or needs. That is why it is critical to associate efforts with the organizational goals and objectives whenever possible.

Standardization is essential because it allows you to compare all the various requests equally and weigh them by their relationship to critical outside elements. The best-run centers of excellence are typically not autonomous in applying their resources. Having that power would not be profitable for a center of excellence. Why? The people who make requests for the services of a center of excellence will quite frequently outrank the person who leads it. If that requester believes they can "pull rank" and tell the person, "My project is priority number one," it will be challenging to prioritize the projects your center of excellence undertakes correctly.

Gating requests

We have helped various organizations implement a well-defined resource allocation process that has streamlined the escalation and proper estimation of critical requests and the proper moderation, gating, and prioritization of technical or process improvement requests. This tried-and-true methodology, used in various government agencies and corporate environments we have worked with, has also virtually eliminated the in-fighting previously associated with the selection and execution of these requests. The following text summarizes that methodology.

Objective: A leadership committee or center of excellence prioritization team should gate, rank, and approve or defer the application of resources toward process improvement requests.

If possible, this committee or team should include one member from each of the various vital disciplines within the organization (customer service, finance, sales, marketing, C-Suite, etc.). That division's point is to allow the departments and department heads to argue amongst themselves versus arguing with the center of excellence. If you provide people with limited resources, they will self-manage their priorities and ensure that the center of excellence invests its time in the organization's agreed priorities. The items the team has decided on will be the requests that gain resources versus a subjective process under the control of the process improvement leaders themselves or those who best intimidate them.

It should be abundantly clear that members of this team have no rank within it. A member of the finance team has the same standing as the member from the c-suite, at least within the function of this group. If the team is not flattened in this way, one member may overpower the group and guide them down the path of their own preference rather than the correct path for the business.

Before we ask our "leadership committee" to approve, disapprove, or prioritize any requested projects, we must prepare them for neutral evaluation and give them an unbiased score in various categories. While we have discussed the items we need top have included with a request, we now need to consider how to evaluate those requests independently.

Standardized requests should be scored as follows:

- What is the process team's estimated cost (for the effort to address the request)?
    o What is the confidence score for that cost? (This can be objective or subjective depending on the maturity of your center of excellence or the quality of the request).
- What is the estimated (financial or other) benefit?
    o What is the confidence score for that benefit?
- What corporate goals is the request aligned with?

Once this initial scoring has been completed, it's time to review the requests and set priorities.

It is not required but highly recommended that all requests appearing to be good candidates for full approval and the application of significant resources be first approved as a "prototype" with a rapid or short-term "report back" deliverable. In other words, you want someone to invest a few days into discovery and build or model a simple prototype to report back with empirical data on the following items:

- Have the confidence score on cost and benefit increased or decreased?
- Have the expected costs or benefits increased or decreased due to this further exploration?
- Are the expected recipients of the improvement excited about the potential change they have seen in a prototype, model, or mockup? (In other words, will this be a helpful or resistant group?)

Your COE (Center of Excellence) facilitator can now present that same prototype, model, or mockup to the leadership committee, helping them validate they will be getting what they expect.

That is a straightforward and high-level overview of the process of gating requests, but there must be a process in place. Otherwise, people will believe that their requests will be addressed in the order they were received, based on their title or rank, or subjectively perceived pain. In this case, a center of excellence has to do its own prioritization, and the team will quickly begin to lose favor across the organization as people who wait longer for their requests will start to perceive the center of excellence as either slow or unresponsive.

In contrast, the center of excellence must be seen as a highly productive and capable internal resource that is limited or constrained and, therefore, competitively allocated. It is neither a lottery nor a system of favoritism. Instead, a requestor must make a good business case for their problem and have a team ready to help embrace the change for their request to reach the top of the stack and gain approval.

Operating the Center of Excellence

Choosing the right facilitator for your center of excellence is critical. Someone familiar with process and change management must be able to facilitate less experienced requestors. They will need to help people understand the procedures they will encounter when they make a request. One or more individuals with this skill set should also be available for prototyping. They become an internal consultant available to the organizational units or department leaders who are making or considering the requests. They will engage with those stakeholders, both internal and external, to help them build prototypes, models, or mockups -should a request reach that stage. Therefore, they must be proficient at discovery. They must be comfortable working with people of various ranks, process proficiency, and be good communicators. Verbal communications are critical for discovery meetings, and written communications are essential to the output of these efforts. Prototypes can be simple wireframes (or diagrammed mockups), but a certain level of tech-savviness is required for someone in this critical role.

The totality of all we have discussed may sound like a lot to take on, and if you are just getting started, it is. The lean and agile process you should start with is much lighter. We are just giving you a more extended-term plan for dealing with the increased demand once the word gets out about what a difference your new center of excellence delivers.

When a process improvement effort has gained approval, the work within it should be as lean and agile as possible, and, as we cover in many places elsewhere in this book, getting started is about gathering the right people and allowing success to snowball. These suggestions around how to gate and staff your center of excellence will be most appropriate once that snowball has begun to gain mass. Suppose the frustrated masses who once despaired of the impossibility of positive change now believe that real change is possible. In that case, they will likely line up with torches and pitchforks, demanding to be next. That is why a process must be implemented to help gate, prioritize, and professionally address these requests.

Another organization (Company Y) we have seen build a successful center of excellence divided its COE into several groups. That does not mean every organization must have full-time people for those groups. It is reasonably practicable for people with a full-time job within an organization to also serve as a critical member of a center of excellence. It all comes down to the need or the value delivered. Suppose your organization can save millions of dollars annually by defining and clearing a backlog of process improvement requests. In that case, spending a few hundred thousand dollars annually to assign dedicated people to those tasks makes perfect sense and brings a high ROI. Likewise, suppose the budget is not available to invest in those kinds of things, but there are a few particular process improvements that would free up the funds needed to build a team. In that case, it may make sense to have process-minded people with other primary responsibilities take those initial projects on as "other duties as assigned."

That is what we saw at "Company Y." People who had various specialties, such as analytics, sales, customer data expertise, privacy compliance, etc., were organized into part-time or on-demand teams that were able to put roughly one day per week into process improvement efforts as a team. Once the process improvement had been completed and the hoped-for ROI achieved, the organization asked one of those people to take over the center of excellence full-time. In turn, they began recruiting other part-time resources from within the organization as their success and value continued to increase.

Looking back at this organization a few years later, they have teams that address systemic change (new applications, new machinery, etc.) and operational change (process, work management, data management, flow, etc.). Each may have one or more full-time resources and a variety of part-time contributors from across the organization engaged for any specific request. This model is particularly effective because those key individuals are aware of the organization's overall ground rules regarding data management (privacy concerns, role-based access, etc.). These dedicated process improvement resources bring continuity across efforts while bringing in SMEs (Subject Matter Experts) from the various operational areas where a change has been deemed beneficial.

In challenging economic times, an organization may be tempted to look at a center of excellence as a potentially disposable resource. However, it is during challenging economic times (provided the organization is large enough to support this role in the first place) that keeping a center of excellence in place may become even more critical.

In favorable economic conditions, a leadership committee may be able to approve performance or process improvement requests based on organizational goals and objectives. Still, they may be forced to prioritize requests based on urgent or critical needs during down conditions.

Consider an organization that must downsize. If an organization has a 10% operating margin in a market that drops by 10%, they may be forced to drop more than 10% of their staff to remain viable. If they have to drop 20% of the staff that manages a particular process while the demand for the output of that process has only dropped by 10%, they have increased the pressure on that process and their organization as a whole.

One thing you don't want to do during a downturn is destabilize outcomes. When times are tough, they are not only challenging for you but also difficult for your customers. They expect the same results if they are still paying you the same price or more. Your hungry competitor may be offering them even better results if they switch. If you want to defend against that, you'd better be able to continue improving the areas you discover are under pressure as you navigate the headwinds.

The true purpose of a center of excellence is to ensure that change within an organization is achieved consistently and predictably. The best practices around determining change-ready champions are always critical. The best practices around communications are also crucial. The experience and lessons your organization has gained include the unique kinds of change that can be affected quickly within your operations and which types require more effort than anyone expects. Remember, the idea of a center of excellence is to ensure that every process improvement within your organization benefits from these valuable lessons again without having to learn them from scratch.

A process improvement center of excellence is not where the answers are. Your process improvement center of excellence team does not have those answers. They are the keepers of the best practices and questions that lead to finding those answers and ensuring that change is effective. They are the keepers of the process by which requests are evenly and fairly scored. They are the keepers of the process by which those requests are reviewed, prototyped, and, if successful, eventually fully designed, documented, and ultimately deployed. They are the facilitators who bring organizational knowledge and best practices to bear within a variable team of SMEs assembled to address requested changes.

What difference does a center of excellence make?

We have observed organizations while they have developed and organized these disciplines, and we have then watched them outperform their competitors who did not create or adopt these disciplines by a factor of 2 to 3 times along various metrics:

- An organization with a trusted center of excellence will be able to make an effective change in as little as one-third of the time that an organization that does not have a center of excellence will take to complete a roughly equal process improvement.
- An organization with a center of excellence is more than three times as likely to have each process improvement effort viewed as a success by the contributors who will work within the process once the effort has been completed.
- We at HighGear have observed an organization with a center of excellence will typically achieve significantly better operational performance improvement than organizations that start from scratch with each effort -for obvious reasons.
- Organizations operating a center of process improvement excellence will typically complete process improvements and/or standardization efforts for 20 to 30 times as many organizational processes as those without a formal center of excellence.
- As established and cited previously in the book, from numerous sources, the number of agile process improvements or standardizations an organization implements is correlated to its performance and long-term sustainability.

- As corporate environments grapple with the most significant wave of baby boomer retirements between now and roughly 2030, those organizations with a high degree of process standardization have a far easier time onboarding younger workers than organizations that scramble to convey human competence from a retiring worker's body of knowledge to an inexperienced replacement. More digitally mature competitors have already built organizational best practices that guide younger workers through delivering the consistent results of their predecessors.

The Center Of Excellence Library

As we wrap up, here is a short list of some of the items we have seen get standardized within a process improvement center of excellence:

- Centralized communication and messaging for the submission and management of process improvement requests and efforts
- Clear multi-year plans (to include defined "tour of duty" statements) for how a center will scale over time
- The creation and operation of a data governance committee and reference documents, e.g.,
  - What will we call a "client" in all of our systems?
  - What date and time formats will we support, and should they all be stored behind the scenes using a standard format such as UTC?
  - How can someone determine if we already have a standard naming convention (or preferred storage location) for what they think might be a new data type?
- Provide help documentation and training aid guidelines:
  - demos
  - user guides
  - videos
  - job aids
  - etc.
- Standardize process improvement tools and techniques:
  - Discovery question banks or "must ask" considerations
  - Data collection tools

- o Wireframing or prototype development tools
- o etc.
- Thought leadership – set and share your vision, market, and promote to others
  - o Internal webinars to educate on the possibilities of process improvement
  - o Education and resources for simplifying the request for COE services
- Track and report – data proves out and delivers your ROI
  - o Metrics models for determining the empirical benefits of continuous process improvement
  - o Report formats to standardize the delivery of ROI projections and post-implementation reports
- Internal and external field trips.
  - o Compare and contrast your process with others.
  - o Study how other firms' standardized processes and process improvement efforts compare with your own.
- Assemble a Super User Group or Committee
  - o Set up an open forum where key users can regularly meet to share best practices and constructive feedback and to review and discuss ongoing process improvement efforts.
  - o Use this group as a recruiting ground for the champions of continuous improvement.

APPENDIX ONE

The Team with the Best People Wins –
Including Process Improvement

In any process improvement effort, people are the most critical element in determining whether your process changes succeed or fail. The people who plan and implement the process change must be intelligent, motivated, and able to understand your business goals and existing processes. And the people who work within those processes must be unified, supportive, and willing to change. If either group is comprised of low performers or people who don't care about the organization's goals, it will be nearly impossible to implement successful organizational change.

That means you can dramatically improve your chance of success (and make your job much easier) if you find the right people and align them with your organization's goals, values, and culture. If you already have those people in your organization, your process improvement work will be much easier. Be sure to engage them in the change efforts so they can help you design good processes, implement them well, and help all your other people follow along.

What if you don't already have those people on your team? Maybe you are hiring for a newly created Center of Excellence. Or maybe your organization struggles to change, and you must bring in new blood. How can you make sure that the new hires will be effective?

Why it is vital to hire the right people

We all know that having good people on your team makes everything easier. But why is it so essential to avoid hiring people who don't fit your team?

If you hire someone who won't apply the intelligence or motivation necessary to implement process change, your change efforts will fail before they start. You will likely find them working on the wrong problems or moving too slowly. The result will be an erosion of organizational trust that change can be accomplished.

If you hire someone who doesn't have people skills, your change efforts may fail because they won't be able to convince the organization to follow the new and better path.

But there is a worse possibility. If you hire someone who doesn't share your organization's values or only cares about their own success, your change efforts will fail, **and** that person will damage the trust and morale of the team around them. That damage can take months or years to repair.

In all those cases, you have to manage the person you hired. You must spend time trying to align them to the organization and even more time trying to improve their performance. And if it doesn't work, you must have that difficult conversation to let them know they will be leaving while you start the search for their replacement. These things take a long time, consume your energy, and damage your team.

Alternatively, you could slow down and work hard to find a good employee who will support their team and make your change projects successful. During a diligent hiring process, you may feel like you are wasting time and delaying important process improvement work. While your projects may be delayed while you search for the right team member, you will be maximizing the chance that they will be successful. And you will also make your team more unified, trustworthy, and capable.

The right mindset

Because of the pressure to hire people, many managers rush the decision. Maybe their team is overloaded, or perhaps they worry that they'll lose their open req (an "open req" is a common shorthand for a "staffing requirement" that has been approved to fill). Whatever the cause, their focus is on their need to hire someone, not the quality of the candidate. With this mindset, they often miss out on candidates' weaknesses and warning signs.

The first step to preventing this problem is to correct your mindset. Don't be afraid of missing the perfect candidate – no one is perfect, but plenty of good candidates are out there. Instead, do everything you can to avoid hiring the wrong person.

Next, determine what skills and attributes you genuinely need for this role. For example, if they will be responsible for designing a new process and training end users, you may need someone with good emotional intelligence. Or, if your new system needs to integrate with several legacy software tools, you may need someone with experience working with those other or older tools. Finally, no matter what skills and attributes you require, you must also identify your team's values and culture to ensure the candidate you hire will fit those values.

Next, you must look for reasons to say no at every stage. It is easy to find reasons to hire a candidate. They aim to get the job and will work hard to show you how great they are! You need to think deeply, ask probing questions, and carefully decide whether the candidate will fit your team and your business needs. If there is a reason to say no at every stage, you should stop interviewing that candidate.

If you have doubts after your first phone call, say no. If your team expresses concerns, say no. Say no if you aren't sure they can learn your business or processes quickly enough. Say NO if you catch yourself trying to justify their weaknesses by pointing to a different strength!

Do not hire someone until you have interviewed them thoroughly and have found no reasons to say no.

How to evaluate candidates

There are countless models for interviewing candidates. We have tried many of them, and so have our clients. Only two have proven to be consistently effective:

Behavioral Interviewing
-    Skills Testing

Neither can stand on its own. However, when used together, they give a comprehensive and accurate understanding of candidates' fit for a job and the organization they will join and serve.

Behavioral interview questions

The first tool is behavioral interviewing. Behavioral interview questions are precisely tailored to elicit real stories from the candidate's past, allowing you to ask probing questions to learn about their actions and decisions during that time. That will give you a more accurate understanding of the candidate than hypothetical questions like "How would you respond if a customer had a problem?"

Here is an example behavioral interview question:

- Tell me about a time you worked with a product support team to resolve a complex problem for a customer. How did you help them fix the problem? How did you ensure the customer stayed happy?

Note there are two parts to this question. The first part instructs the candidate to tell a real story about a time when they were in a specific situation. Anyone who is a good fit for your job will have plenty of stories to answer your question. Even if they haven't been in the exact situation you describe, they can share a similar story and explain how it is connected.

The second part asks specific questions about what you want to know. These tell the candidate what kind of story to choose from their history and what they should highlight in their story.

Finally, there is a third component: deep follow-up questions. As the candidate tells their story, you must actively listen and ask probing questions about it. Please don't wait until the end of their answer and then ask, interrupt them, and ask them to clarify anything you need to know. In the example question above, they might say they decided to escalate the problem to the support manager. Instead of assuming you know why they did that, ask them to explain it. They may surprise you! You may learn that they always escalate to the manager, which could tell you they do not prioritize problems effectively. Or they may say that this was the third time in a month that this customer had a problem, which could show you that they understand the risks of repeated failures. Keep asking follow-up questions and digging deeper until you are sure that you understand their actions and decisions in that story because you are using them to evaluate their demonstrated behaviors – as they are soon to be the behaviors you will be responsible for should you hire them.

Skill tests

The second tool is objective skill tests. Every job requires different tests, but you should always test the most critical skills. These tests may be time-consuming for the candidate, so we usually do them after they have completed the behavioral interviews and we feel confident that we want to hire them.

For example, at HighGear, our software engineers do a take-home programming test that takes 6-8 hours. It is a simplified version of a few key technical details that our software requires. After they submit their completed program, we meet with them on a video call to review the code and ask them questions. This test is not difficult, but it is complex enough to clearly show the candidate's programming skills (or lack thereof).

Our sales, marketing, and customer service candidates do a take-home test of a different sort. Because HighGear is a no-code solution that enables anyone to automate their business processes, anyone we hire should be able to build a process in HighGear. So we have them watch 2 hours of HighGear training videos and then give them another 6 hours to create a basic HighGear process. Once they complete that, we do a video call to review what they built and ask some questions. Again, this test is designed not to be difficult, but it clearly shows whether the candidate will succeed if they join our team and need to learn our product more deeply.

You can see that creating these tests requires some work. You may be able to find a testing vendor that already has standard tests for the skills you need. Most likely, you will need to build your own tests. That can be a lot of work, and you must iterate several times before your tests are simple enough and accurate enough. But this effort will pay off the first time it saves you from hiring a friendly, experienced, and polished candidate who can't actually do the work required.

Making a decision

After you have gathered all of this information, how do you decide? If four people interviewed the candidate, how do you all get on the same page?

Before we move on to the skills tests, we conduct a standardized interview results meeting for each candidate. We do this as soon as possible after their interviews are complete so our evaluations are fresh. Each interviewer must attend the meeting and come prepared to recommend either "Hire" or "Don't Hire." The final decision is the hiring manager's. However, forcing every interviewer to make an explicit hire/don't hire decision (before sharing various other extraneous opinions about the person they interviewed) helps them clarify their thinking and make a better recommendation. To support their recommendation, each interviewer offers brief feedback about the candidate's fit in three categories: interpersonal, cultural, and skills. If four people each say "Hire" or "Don't Hire" and then spend two minutes explaining their recommendation, you can finish an interview results meeting in 10 minutes. That is an incredibly effective use of time, and the discipline of doing it will pay off greatly as you make better hires – or, more importantly, stop making bad hires.

Additional Resources

HighGear derived much of our hiring process guidance from the Manager Tools podcast. Their website is www.manager-tools.com. They offer a treasure trove of practical tools and educational resources for managers. Here are some specific podcast episodes that are particularly helpful for improving your hiring process and making better hiring decisions:

- Effective Hiring: Set the Bar High
- https://www.manager-tools.com/2007/04/
  effective-hiring-set-the-bar-high
- How to Prepare to Interview Someone
- https://www.manager-tools.com/2007/06/
  how-to-prepare-for-an-interview
- How to Create a Simple Behavioral Interview
  Questions
- https://www.manager-tools.com/2008/06/
  how-to-create-a-simple-behavioral-interview-question
- The First Rule of Probing In an Interview
- https://www.manager-tools.com/2012/01/
  first-rule-probing-interview
- The Interview Results Capture Meeting
- https://www.manager-tools.com/2008/04/
  the-interview-results-capture-meeting
- Deciding Between Two Good Candidates
- http://www.manager-tools.com/2009/03/
  deciding-between-two-good-candidates
- How to Write a Job Advertisement
- https://www.manager-tools.com/2011/02/
  write-a-job-advertisement-part-1
- https://www.manager-tools.com/2011/02/
  write-a-job-advertisement-part-2
- Questions to Ask Candidate References
- https://www.manager-tools.com/2013/06/
  questions-ask-references-check-part-1
- https://www.manager-tools.com/2013/06/questions-
  ask-candidate-references-part-2-hall-fame-guidance
- How to Make a Job Offer
- https://www.manager-tools.com/2007/05/
  how-to-make-a-job-offer-part-1-of-2

- https://www.manager-tools.com/2007/05/
  how-to-make-a-job-offer-part-2-of-2
- Conduct Multiple Interviews
- https://www.manager-tools.com/2011/01/
  conduct-multiple-interviews-chapter-1-part-1
- https://www.manager-tools.com/2011/01/
  conduct-multiple-interviews-chapter-1-part-2
- https://www.manager-tools.com/2011/01/
  conduct-multiple-interviews-chapter-1-part-3
- Evaluating People on Your Bench
- https://www.manager-tools.com/2012/03/
  bench-evaluation-chapter-1-probing

Data Capture Tools

As a helpful resource, we have provided several basic tools for facilitating the discovery process. While we would always suggest that process improvement done in HighGear will be better and faster, the tools provided do not require you to be a HighGear client to use them.

You can download these and other tools via:
https://www.TheProcessOfImprovement.com

Defining Operational Excellence

We offer several expanded definitions of Operational Excellence and the underlying components on our website, including a video overview of the topic.

You can access these resources via:

https://www.TheProcessOfImprovement.com.,
or via scanning the QR code on the last page of this book.

Scan here to access additional resources related to this book.

www.ingramcontent.com/pod-product-compliance
Lightning Source LLC
Chambersburg PA
CBHW022102210326
41518CB00039B/362